A *The* POSTLES
of JESUS

D1554621

By the same author . . .
Commentary on Mark

The
Apostles
of Jesus

J. D. Jones

KREGEL PUBLICATIONS
Grand Rapids, Michigan 49501

The Apostles of Jesus by J. D. Jones © 1992 by Kregel Publications, P.O. Box 2607, Grand Rapids, Michigan 49501. Formerly published as *The Glorious Company of the Apostles* in 1904 by James Clarke and Co., London and *The Apostles of Christ* by Klock and Klock in 1982. All rights reserved. Those Scriptures marked NIV are taken from the Holy Bible, New International Version, used by permission.

Cover photo: Art Jacobs
Cover and book design: Al Hartman

Library of Congress Cataloging-in-Publication Data

Jones, J. D. (John Daniel), 1865-1942.
   The apostles of Jesus: studies in the character of the twelve/ J.D. Jones.
       p.   cm.
   1. Apostles—Biography.   2. Bible. N.T.—Biography. I. Title.
BS2440.J66   1992   225.9'22—dc20   91-22663
[B]   CIP

ISBN 0-8254-2971-4

   1 2 3 4 5 printing/year 96 95 94 93 92

Printed in the United States of America

CONTENTS

Foreword 7
Prefatory Note 9

1. The Apostles 11
2. Peter 21
3. James 33
4. John 45
5. Andrew 55
6. Philip 65
7. Bartholomew 75
8. Matthew 85
9. Thomas 95
10. Simon the Zealot 107
11. The Unknown Apostles 117
12. Judas Iscariot 127

FOREWORD

JOHN WOODEN WILL probably be remembered as the greatest coach in the history of basketball. His pattern of success, from his humble beginnings in Indiana to ten Pacific Eight Conference championships in twelve years, became the envy of every other basketball coach in the country.

What set Wooden apart from the others? By what means did he instill in the hearts and minds of UCLA's basketball team the desire to be champions?

John Wooden was a leader. He was never known for his recruiting, but he possessed the ability to work and shape different kinds of players. He won with tall men such as Abdul-Jabbar and Walton, and he won with men of much smaller stature as well. He won with teams of incredible talent, and he won with teams of modest talent. The last team he coached looked as if it would place no better than third, yet they beat top-ranked Kentucky in the finals.

Two emphases in John Wooden's teaching/learning routine were modeling and communication. Players learned from the way in which he stimulated patterned-offense drills or half-court scrimmages with his body. He not only demonstrated the correct way to perform each action, but learned what was incorrect as well. His communication was equally as clear. He knew each player's name and used it. His instructions, compliments, or expressions of displeasure, were audible and authoritative, clear and concise.

Wooden made no provision for "grandstanders." To a reporter he said:

"Some players who were individual stars in high school were eager, when they came to UCLA to dramatize their skill by fancy ballhandling, jazzy dribbling, and behind-the-back or blind passing. They quickly learned that 'showboating' was forbidden. *Team work* was the name of the game."

It was clear to each player that John Wooden was deeply concerned about him. And so year-by-year he took a group of diverse young men and, through his own method of leadership, welded them into a winning team.

The Lord Jesus Christ did the same. He took a group of the most unlikely people from divergent walks of life, and made them into "the glorious company of the apostles." He enthused into them the desire to go out and change the world by preaching the Gospel. During His time with them He modeled for them the kind of life they should lead, and as He preached and taught the people He illustrated from them the kind of message they were to proclaim.

The essence of the Lord Jesus' ministry has been captured for us by John Daniel Jones (1865-1942), a Welsh preacher who ministered in Bournemouth, England, for thirty-nine years. He was honored for his work with doctorates from the Universities of St. Andrews, Manchester, and Wales. His church was crowded Sunday by Sunday by people who were attracted to his preaching and method of expounding the Word.

Dr. Jones faithfully served the Free Churches of England. He held high offices in different ecclesiastical bodies, including being Moderator of the International Congregational Council and President of the National Free Church Council. In these capacities he had the opportunity to work closely with leaders of different kinds.

His knowledge of human nature, the principles of leadership, and how to draw the best out of people, all find expression in his timely study of the *The Apostles of Jesus.* Formerly published under the title, *The Glorious Company of the Apostles: Being Studies in the Characters of the Twelve,* this treatment deserves to be read carefully, for we have much to learn from "The Twelve," and, as the Apostle Paul pointed out "not many wise according to the flesh, not many mighty, not many noble" are called to become Christians. And seeing God has chosen the foolish things of the world to shame the wise, and the weak to expose the limitations of the strong, we should consider how the Lord Jesus Christ molded the first of His disciples; for we, like them, have been called to spread the same message. We have much to learn, therefore, from these perceptive studies.

Cyril J. Barber, Author, *The Minister's Library*

Prefatory Note

The sermons contained in this volume were originally delivered on consecutive Sabbath mornings in the regular course of my ministry at Richmond Hill. They are essentially *spoken* sermons, and they have been printed exactly as they were spoken. I have derived help from various quarters in the preparation of these "Studies," especially from Dr. Alexander Whyte's *Bible Characters,* and Dr. A. B. Bruce's beautiful book, *The Training of the Twelve.* My thanks are due to the Rev. A. J. Pearse, M.A., of Trowbridge, for valued counsel and help, and to my friend, Mr. E. Carr, who has added to previous kindnesses by undertaking all the work connected with the passing of this volume through the press.

J. D. Jones

Editor's Note: Some changes have been made in the original text to make the book more readable to a new generation of readers. Also, the sermon texts at the beginning of each chapter have been taken from the Holy Bible, New International Version.

1

THE APOSTLES

*"He appointed twelve—designating them apostles—that they might
be with him and that he might send them out to preach."*
—Mark 3:14 NIV

I HAVE LONG had it in mind to preach a series of sermons upon those
twelve men whom Christ honored by calling out of the whole
multitude of His disciples to be His chosen friends—the twelve men
who are known throughout the Christian Church as "the glorious
company of the Apostles." I have desired to do this for at least two
reasons. *First,* because by studying the characters of the men whom
Christ selected to be His intimates and chief associates, we are certain
to learn something about the character and aims of our Lord Himself.
And, *second,* because the Apostles are well worth knowing for their
own sakes.

"Great men taken up in any way," says Carlyle, "are profitable
company. We cannot look, however imperfectly, upon a great man
without gaining something by him." Now when we associate with
the Apostles of Jesus Christ, we company not simply with great men,
but we join with the *greatest* of men. Yes, I will make bold to say that
amongst those born of women there are none greater than the holy
and blessed twelve.

When we are in the society of the Apostles we are in the *best*
society, and it is simply impossible for us to make friends of Peter and
James and John and Andrew and the rest without gaining something
by them, without catching from them something of that zeal and

11

devotion and sacrificial love which engraved their names on the foundations of the New Jerusalem, and have set them on twelve thrones judging the twelve tribes of Israel.

Before I proceed to deal with the individuals who compose the "glorious company," however, there are certain preliminary questions that need to be briefly discussed, and there are certain general remarks applying to the Apostolate as a whole that should be made.

The Reasons for the Calling of the Twelve

First of all, let us look at the reasons why Jesus called the twelve. Those reasons seem to be at least three in number: (1) From the way in which the verse of my text is worded I should gather that one reason why Jesus called the twelve was that *He needed human sympathy.* "He appointed twelve," says Mark, "that they might be with Him." Nothing is more touching in the record of our Lord's life than His hunger for human sympathy. Take the supreme and critical hour of all as an illustration. When He agonized beneath the burden of the world's sin in Gethsemane, in the very midst of His distress He returned to the place where He had left Peter and James and John. To touch a friendly hand, to hear a friendly voice, would have been a help to Jesus just then. But when He came, He found them sleeping.

"Could ye not watch with Me one hour?" Jesus asked them. And in that sorrowful reproach there is the cry of a heart faint for human sympathy. Yes, all through life Christ craved sympathy. He longed for loving and trusty friends. He was only in the early stages of His career at this time. But already it had become evident to Him that it was a sorrowful way He had to tread. If you will only turn back to Mark 2:1 you will see that the authorities had declared against Him. Already priests and elders and scribes had begun to thwart, to oppose, to persecute Him. Even as early as this Jesus read rejection as His fate. And true man as He was, He longed for a few real and honest souls who would befriend Him, whatever might happen. And so He appointed twelve "that they might be with Him." And the faithful sympathy of the twelve went to His very heart. "Ye are they," He said, with loving gratitude in the upper room on the night before He died, "ye are they which have continued with Me in My temptations."

(2) Another and more important reason for the calling of the twelve was this—Christ *needed help in His work.* Up to this point Jesus had been working alone. His preaching had created great excitement, and the people crowded to hear Him, but of necessity His labors had been confined to a small area. It was only a few towns in Galilee that had enjoyed the privilege of hearing Him preach. But wherever Christ looked, He saw people hungering for the Gospel He had brought. "The harvest truly is plenteous," He said, "but the laborers are few." Just as in later days Barnabas, finding the work at Antioch becoming too much for him, sent to Tarsus for Paul; just as John Wesley wrote from Georgia to George Whitefield, saying, "Only Mr. Delamotte is with me, till God shall stir up the hearts of some of His servants, who, putting their lives in their hands, shall come over and help us where the harvest is so great and the laborers are so few. What if thou art the man, Mr. Whitefield?" So now, to cope with the growing work, Jesus summoned these twelve men that they might be with Him, and that He might send them forth to preach.

(3) The third reason for the calling of the twelve was this: Christ was taking forethought for *the continuance of His work after He was gone.* Most of us have seen Holman Hunt's great picture, "The Shadow of the Cross." The suggestion of the painter is that the shadow of the Cross lay upon the soul of Jesus and His mother Mary, even while they were still together in the carpenter's shop at Nazareth. How far the painter is right I cannot tell. But this I know, that by the time Christ came to call His twelve Apostles, the shadow of the Cross was already lying cold and heavy upon His heart. He knew that the prophet's word was to be fulfilled, and that He was to be despised and rejected of men.

Seeing death in front of Him, Christ took measures to perpetuate and extend His work. This was how He did it: He appointed twelve that they might be with Him. Most men seek to perpetuate their influence by putting the truth they have to teach into writing. Plato wrote his *Republic*, Aristotle his *Philosophy*, Dante his great poem on *Purgatory* and *Hell* and *Paradise*, Shakespeare his *King Lear* and his *Hamlet*, Milton his *Paradise Lost.*

But Christ never wrote a single line. Instead of writing books, He chose the twelve. Christ's greatest gift to the world was not His words, but *Himself!* The Gospel is not so much in what He *said*, as in what He *was* and *did.* So He appointed twelve that they might be with Him; that they might not only hear His wondrous words, but might see His glorious life and behold His mighty works, and weep at His Cross and exult at His empty grave, and so become His witnesses in Jerusalem and to the uttermost parts of the earth.

The Number Twelve

"And He appointed twelve." It was not by chance or accident that Christ appointed twelve—no more, no less. That there were others eligible for this high dignity is evident from the fact that shortly afterwards Christ found seventy fitted to be sent forth to preach His Holy Gospel. It was by no accident, but of deliberation and set purpose that Christ chose twelve. The number is significant and symbolical. "He appointed twelve," says Dr. Chadwick, "in clear allusion to the tribes of a new Israel, a spiritual circumcision, another peculiar people."

By that choice of twelve Christ did two things: He made a stupendous claim for Himself. Every Jew knew in a moment what that choice of twelve implied. It implied that Jesus was the promised and long-expected Messiah. It meant that He was the fulfillment of ancient prophecy. It meant that all the glowing visions of a world-wide kingdom of righteousness and peace, given to the world by seer and Psalmist—the seventy-second Psalm, the Isaiah eleven, sixty, and sixty-five—all those blessed predictions on which the Jews had built all their hopes, had found their realization in Jesus Christ.

One further thing the choice of this number twelve did. It provided the Apostles themselves with a constant "stimulus to devotion and support of faith." The very number twelve would carry their minds back to the promises, to that word of the Lord which stands sure. It would be to them what the figurative names of their children were to the prophets, what the bones of Joseph were to the enslaved Israelites, a stimulus to their drooping and halting faith.

There were rough and troubled days in front of these men, days of gloom and apparently hopeless defeat. Christ gave them this number to remind them of the kingdom the Gospel of which they were sent to preach. This was that glorious kingdom to the establishment of which God, by the mouth of Psalmist and prophet, had again plighted His holy and inviolable word.

"And He appointed twelve, that they might be with Him." Then Mark proceeds to give us the names of the twelve so appointed. As I read the list, two verses of Scripture suggest themselves to me as the best commentary upon this list of names.

"Not Many Noble"

The first verse that suggests itself to me as I read the names of the twelve is that verse which you will find in Paul's first letter to the Corinthians, "Not many wise, not many mighty, not many noble are called." I look through this list, and I cannot find in it the name of a single nobleman; I cannot find in it the name of a single rabbi; I cannot find in it the name of a single honorable counselor; I cannot find in it the name of a single person of wealth or position.

What I *do* find are fishermen, publicans and outlaws. In very truth as I read this list I am constrained to say that it was the foolish things of the world, and the weak things of the world, and the base things of the world, and the things that are despised, yea, and the things that are not, that Christ chose when He appointed these twelve—including Peter the fisherman, and Matthew the tax-gatherer, Simon the ex-rebel—that they might be with Him.

Why, it has been asked, did Christ choose fishermen and publicans for His apostles? The true answer is probably the one Dr. A. B. Bruce gives in *The Training of the Twelve*. Jesus had to be content with fishermen and publicans and zealots for disciples because "they were the best that could be had." It was not that Christ would not accept the cultured and the well-born. That would be to make the Christ a class-conscious Christ. And as a matter of fact and history, at a later stage Christ called to the Apostolate Saul of Tarsus, a Jew of purest blood, a Hebrew of the Hebrews, and the very flower of culture. No, Jesus called these humble, obscure, peasant folk to be His Apostles because they were the best that could be had.

Those who thought themselves better than they, were too proud to become Apostles. Nicodemus, the great Rabbi, had some kind of hesitating belief in Christ; Joseph of Arimathaea, the honorable Counselor, was a secret disciple. But neither Nicodemus nor Joseph loved Jesus well enough to sacrifice position and place and power for His sake. For those who were ready to "leave all and follow Him," Jesus had to look to these men of humble and lowly station, but men who had honest, believing, and sacrificial hearts.

I believe Christ chose these lowly men for His Apostles because they were the best that could be had. But when I think further about them, I feel inclined to add that better men than these could not possibly have been chosen. For, in the first place, poverty and lowly station are no hindrance to religious usefulness. Life, as you ascend, tends to become more and more artificial. Often enough we gain our culture and our acquaintance with the world's ways at the expense of our innocence and guilelessness of heart, so that in every age it has been true that God reveals to babes what He hides from the wise and prudent.

To speak to the great heart of humanity, to its great primitive wants and sorrows, these plain, unsophisticated peasants of Galilee were far better fitted than the most learned of Jerusalem rabbis; and, in the second place, history demonstrates that spiritual power does not depend upon noble birth or high culture.

I am not depreciating culture. I believe in an educated ministry, and if I had my way I would equip every minister with the highest possible culture. But facts prove beyond controversy or dispute that spiritual power in no way depends upon culture, and that from the ranks of humble and uneducated men spiritual geniuses may come.

Dwight L. Moody, that great evangelist, a man of immense spiritual power, sprang from a humble home, and was ignorant of letters and had never learned. Charles Haddon Spurgeon, the man known as the "Prince of preachers," lacked college training. John Bunyan, the greatest allegorist of Christendom, whose *Pilgrim's Progress* has spoken to the human heart as no other book save the Bible has ever done, was a tinker in the town of Bedford.

These men—fishermen, publicans, zealots—were also spiritual geniuses. By their faith they subdued kingdoms, wrought righteousness, obtained promises, stopped the mouths of lions, quenched the power of fire, escaped the edge of the sword, from weakness were made strong, waxed mighty in war, put to flight armies of aliens, turned the world upside down. Yes, they were the foolish things, and the weak things, and the base things, and the despised things of the world; but they were strong in the Lord, they were rich in faith, they were mighty in prayer, and God used them to put to shame the wise and the strong, and to bring to nought the things that are.

Whosoever Will

The second verse of Scripture that comes to my mind as I read this list is the verse in John's Gospel which says—"Whosoever cometh I will in no wise cast out." If I wanted proof of the universal and all-embracing love of Jesus Christ, this list would suffice me. If I wanted proof that Christ has no favorites, but that people of varying temperament and diverse gifts are equally welcome to Him, this list would suffice me.

When I look down the names I find infinite variety and difference among the appointed twelve. Do you want difference of temperament? Then you have it, say, in Peter and John—Peter the man of action, John the man of prayer. Peter the man of bold, impulsive, eager spirit; John the man of quiet, contemplative, loving heart.

Do you want difference in spiritual gift? You have it, say, in Nathaniel or Bartholomew and Thomas. Nathaniel of a believing soul, and Thomas of a skeptical spirit. Nathaniel was easily ready to say, "Thou art the Son of God, Thou art the King of Israel." Thomas was slow to credit the protests of all his fellow disciples, and said sadly, "Except I shall see in His hands the print of the nails, and put my finger into the print of the nails, and put my hand into His side, I will not believe."

Do you want difference of political opinion? Well, you have it in its most extreme and violent form in the contrast between Matthew and Simon the Canaanite. Matthew the publican, and Simon the Zealot; Matthew the servant of the Roman Government, and Simon the rebel against it. Matthew the tax-gatherer, and Simon the tax-hater. Matthew who wore the uniform of Rome, and Simon who had drawn sword against it.

When I read this list, with its amazing contrasts, with its Peter and its John, with its Bartholomew and its Thomas, with its Matthew and Simon, I know it is true that Christ is willing to receive people into His church and into His service of the most diverse temperament, qualities and gifts. "Whosoever will may come," is written over His Church. There is room in it for white and black, for Englishman and Dutchman, for Catholic and Protestant. There is room in it for people as diverse as Augustine and Telagius, Martin Luther and Ignatius Loyola, George Herbert and John Bunyan, Dr. Pusey and Charles Spurgeon.

"Whosoever will may come" is written over the entrance to His vineyard; there is room, for the person of five talents, and the person of only one; there is room for the man of action, and the man of prayer; there is room for Martha and for Mary; there is room for Dorcas and for Lydia; there is room for the preacher and the teacher, and the singer and the giver; there is room for those who only stand and wait. Yes, there is room for all—Christ welcomes every variety of service. There is room for you and me. Yes—

> You and I in fields so broad
> Some duties may fulfill.

The Object and End of the Calling

Now let me pass on to say a word about the object Christ had in view in calling these twelve men. According to my text, that object was twofold. *First*, He called these twelve that they might be with Him. Christ wanted to teach and to train these men. They were very ignorant and had much to learn, as the Gospels only too plainly show. Christ's first object in calling them out of the multitude of His disciples was that they might be with Him, and by being with Him they might be trained and taught for the work of the Christian Ministry. They were, if I may be allowed so to put it, Christ's apprentices: Just as Joshua was Moses' apprentice, and Samuel was Eli's apprentice, and Timothy was Paul's apprentice, so the twelve were the apprentices of Jesus, called to be with the Master in order that, by living with the Master, they might learn of Him, and so be fitted to carry out His work.

But the end of their calling was not that they might simply be with Jesus: *Second*, Christ called these twelve with the intention of sending them forth to preach. They were to learn of Jesus in order that they might teach others. Their time of fellowship was meant to prepare them for their time of service. They were called to be disciples—or "learners," so that they might become Apostles, "men sent." He appointed twelve that they might be with Him, and that He might send them forth to preach. This leads me to make these two general remarks: (1) *Discipleship* must come before *apostleship*. We must first of all *learn* of Christ, before we can *teach* others about Him. We must be *with* Him before we are fit to preach *about* Him. This is a truth that is perhaps most applicable to those who are in the first flush of their religious enthusiasm. God forbid that I should say a single word to dampen a young convert's zeal, but suffer me to say this with all

Christian kindness: we had better take the position of a *disciple* before we undertake the work of an *apostle*. Christ kept these men with Him *learning* before He sent them forth to preach. And if we spend time in school with Christ, we shall be the better apostles for it. Christ calls us first to be with Him, and only secondly to send us forth.

(2) But if a young convert here and there needs to be reminded that discipleship comes before apostleship—the whole Church almost needs to be reminded that *apostleship* is the end of *discipleship*. These twelve were called to be with Him, *and* that He might send them forth. The end of the *calling* was the *sending*. "And He chose twelve," says Luke in the corresponding account, "whom He named apostles." What does the word apostle mean? It means "one who is sent."

"Even as the Father sent me," said Jesus, "even so send I you." Jesus called Peter and John and James and Andrew and the rest, in order that He might send them forth to go on His errands, to do His work, to preach His Gospel. "Called," says Paul in one of his letters, "to be an Apostle." Called? What to? To privilege? Yes. To honor? Yes. To joy? Yes. But "called" before and above all these—called in order that he might be sent.

Called? What to? To a life of ease and quietness and rest? Oh no! Called in order that he might be sent—sent to preach to the Diana worshipers of Ephesus, and the philosophers of Athens, and the legionaries of Rome. Called to be stoned at Lystra, to be scourged at Philippi, to be imprisoned at Caesarea, to die without the gate—called to be an Apostle, called in order that he might be sent. "Chosen," says Luke of these twelve, "to be Apostles."

Chosen for what? Just to be with Christ, enjoying His sweet and blessed fellowship? No, chosen that they might be sent; saved that they might save others; blessed that they might become a blessing; redeemed that they might preach the Gospel of redemption; chosen that they might bear Christ's name before governors and kings and before the children of Israel, and suffer many things for that Name's sake—chosen in order that they might be sent.

The *calling* and the *sending* still go hand-in-hand. The end of discipleship is apostleship. We delight to think that we have been *called*—called of God! But to what have we been called? Called to fellowship with Christ? Yes, primarily, but that is not the end of our calling. He has appointed us to be with Him *and* that He may send us forth.

We have been called in order that we may be sent to do Christ's work, to run Christ's errands, to proclaim Christ's name. Chosen? Yes, but chosen for what? To fold our arms, and spend our lives in congratulating ourselves that we are saved? Oh, no! but chosen to be Apostles—chosen that we may be sent, saved that we may save others, blessed that we may bless others, entrusted with the glorious Gospel that we may carry it to others.

Have we always remembered this? Have not some of us while rejoicing in the "calling" and the "choosing" forgotten all about the "sending"? Have not some of us been disciples for years without becoming apostles? If there is one thing Christian men and women need to realize today, it is this; discipleship must issue in apostleship. We are called in order that we may be sent—that while chosen for high privilege and glorious honor, we are above all things chosen for strenuous and loving service.

I read a story the other day about a ship which came across another vessel with sails blown away and masts broken. Glasses were brought to bear upon it, but there was no movement on deck, nor, indeed, any sign of life. A boat put off to board and examine the derelict. On the deck in a huddled heap they found one man with sunken cheeks and glassy eyes and bony hands—a mere ruckle of bones—but not dead. They took the starved creature back with them, and when they got him on board they applied restoratives to him, and by and by consciousness returned, and his lips began to move, and those who bent over him caught this whispered sentence: "There is another man—there is another man."

The saved man's first thought was of the other who needed saving. That is how it ought to be with us, and the great Salvation of the Gospel. Saved ourselves, we ought to remember "there is another man," and seek to save him. "That other man," is in the same street with ourselves, next door to ourselves, in the same house with ourselves, and we have not troubled ourselves about him. Let us always remember, "There is another man." Saved ourselves, let us seek to save others. Having found Messiah ourselves, let us tell others about Him. Christ's kingdom will not tarry long when Christian people once realize that discipleship must end in apostleship, and they are called to be sent.

2

PETER

"Then (Andrew) brought Simon to Jesus, who looked upon him and said, 'You are Simon son of John. You will be called Cephas (which, when translated, is Peter).'"   —John 1:42 NIV

IN THE GOSPELS there are to be found three separate and distinct lists of the twelve Apostles. An examination of those lists reveals some variations in the order in which the names of the Apostles are mentioned. The Holy Evangelists are not agreed as to which of the Apostles should be mentioned second, and which third, and which fourth, and which seventh and which eighth, and which tenth and which eleventh. However much they may differ as to intermediate names, however, they are absolutely agreed as to which name should be first and which name should be last. At the end of the lists in Matthew, Mark and Luke will be found the name of Judas—"who also betrayed Him." At the head of all three lists you will find the name of Simon the son of John, who also was surnamed Peter. The place of shame and ignominy and eternal dishonor belongs by universal consent to the traitor; and by an equally clear and indisputable title the place of leadership and primacy belongs to Simon Peter.

It is no accident or mere chance that the name of Simon Peter in every case heads the list of the holy and blessed Twelve. Peter's name comes first because, without controversy or dispute, he was the natural head and leader of the Apostolic company. We may repudiate, and we *do* repudiate, the claims made for Peter by the Roman Church, for the simple reason that they have no shred of support in history or fact. Jesus Christ conferred no spiritual privilege or prerogative on Peter which He did not also bestow upon his associates in the Apostolic College.

Rome bases the stupendous claims she makes for Peter upon the supposition that certain unique powers were conferred upon him by Christ after He had made the great Confession. But in other parts of the New Testament I find the very same power conferred upon the other Apostles. "Upon this Rock," said Christ to Peter on that great day in the Apostle's history, "I will build My Church." But when I turn to the Book of Revelation, I find that it is not upon Peter alone that the Church is built; but the city has *twelve* foundations, and upon those foundations the names of the twelve Apostles of the Lamb.

"Whatsoever thou shalt bind on earth shall be bound in heaven, and whatsoever thou shalt loose on earth shall be loosed in heaven," said Christ to Peter on that same supreme never-to-be-forgotten occasion. But I pass on from the sixteenth to the eighteenth of Matthew, and I find Christ, in precisely identical terms, conferring that same wonderful and mysterious prerogative upon all the twelve.

No! Christ conferred no special or unique powers upon Peter. He bestowed upon him no lordship or authority over his brethren. There is not the slightest shadow of foundation for the Roman theory of an official primacy. But while thus repudiating the Roman claim, I for one frankly and unreservedly admit that Peter did exercise a kind of primacy amongst the twelve. The primacy he exercised was not the primacy of *office*, but the primacy of *character*. Bring any twelve men together, and before they have been in company a week the man of strongest character amongst them—though he be unadorned by any trappings of office, and bear no title of rank or dignity—will inevitably assert himself as leader, and exercise supremacy over the rest.

Simon Peter was by nature a strong, masterful man. He had a certain force and energy of character that fitted him, and inevitably made him a leader of men. Had we but Peter's early history written out for us, I am persuaded we should find that he had been a leader amongst the fishermen of the lake and a leader amongst the townsmen of Bethsaida before he became the leader of the twelve.

Indeed, Peter was the kind of man who would be prominent anywhere, and the very same qualities that made him prominent in the town of Bethsaida and the fishing circles of Galilee, speedily put him in the first place in this glorious company of the Apostles.

That Peter was first among the twelve, no one with the New Testament before him can for a moment doubt. For the Gospels are full of Peter. Yes, next to our Lord, it is of Peter the Gospels most often speak. Of some of the Apostles we know absolutely nothing but their names—preserved for us in the Evangelists' lists. And even of the greatest of the glorious company—of James and John and Andrew—the pictures given to us in the Gospels are dim and shadowy. But the picture of Peter is detailed and vivid and lifelike. That is how we always see Peter—as the leader of the twelve. He asks questions for the twelve; he makes suggestions for the twelve; he expresses opinions in the name of the twelve. The official primacy of the Roman Church we repudiate, but the fact that Peter exercised a primacy among the twelve, springing from his own bold, masterful, and impetuous nature, is a fact written large upon every page of the New Testament.

The Contrasts in Peter's Nature

When I read certain passages in the Gospels, I do not wonder that Peter was acknowledged, without complaint or dispute, as the prince and leader of the twelve, even though a saintly and seraphic John was of the company. For at times Peter is an inspired man, and scales the heavens. He has his moments of rapture and high vision when he is fit to take his place by the side of Moses and David and Isaiah.

When the disciples found that miraculous draught of fishes enclosed within their nets, it was only on Peter's soul that there flashed a new sense of the holiness and majesty of Christ, and of the whole Apostolic company he was the only one to fall at Christ's feet and cry, "Depart from me, for I am a sinful man, O Lord." When after those hard sayings in Capernaum the crowds were deserting Jesus Christ, and He turned to His disciples with the pathetic, heartbreaking question, "Will ye also go away?" it was from Peter's generous and loving soul that there came the great and immortal answer: "Lord, to whom shall we go? Thou hast the words of eternal life."

And when again, in Caesarea, Christ made that wistful inquiry, "Whom say ye that I am?" it was the inspired Peter who made that momentous reply, "Thou art the Christ, the Son of the Living God." Yes, when I read of the incident on the lake, and the answer in Capernaum, and the confession in Caesarea, I do not wonder that the first place amongst the twelve was given to a man of such insight and vision and rapture as this.

But there are other passages in the Gospels which, when I read, I marvel that Peter was among the twelve at all: when I come across those passages in which Peter begins to boast; when I read of his presuming to correct and rebuke the Christ; when I read about his sleeping in the garden; and when I read of that terrible and shameful episode in the Judgment Hall, I marvel that instead of coming down to us as the prince and chief of the Apostles, Peter, the denier and the blasphemer, did not make his bed with Judas the betrayer in the lowest hell.

There are violent and extreme contrasts in the character of Peter. None of the Apostles soared to such heights as he, and none, save the son of perdition, sank to such awful depths. None heard such words of praise from the lips of Christ, and none such terrible words of reproach. Cast your eye over his history. One day we find him winning from Christ the most magnificent eulogy His lips ever pronounced. "Blessed art thou, Simon Bar Jona, for flesh and blood hath not revealed it unto thee, but My Father, which is in heaven." On another we find him provoking from the Lord that most scathing of rebukes, "Get thee behind Me, Satan, thou art a stumbling block upon Me."

At one time you find him the companion of the Savior on the Blessed Mount, on another you find him cursing and swearing he did not know the man. Yes, according to the Gospel Peter was both saint and grievous sinner. Like Paul, he was at times snatched up into the seventh heaven, and, like Dante, at other times he saw hell; one day you find him in the heavenly places in Christ Jesus, and another day you find him in the horrible pit.

Indeed, so startling is the contrast that we could scarcely believe the man of Caesarea and the blasphemer of the Judgment Hall were one and the same person, if we did not carry the confirmation of it in our own experience. We have but to look within and we will know this picture of Peter is drawn from life, for we shall see those same violent, amazing and almost unbelievable contrasts in our own hearts. Is it possible, you say, for a man to behold the glory of the Lord on the Mount and then to forsake Him in the Garden? Is it possible for a man to confess Christ in Caesarea, and then forswear Him in the Judgment Hall?

Yes, it is quite possible. Look into your own hearts, and you will know it is quite possible. For in your own heart you will see both heaven and hell, aspirations and desires born of God, and hideous lusts that issue from the pit. And with heaven and hell in these deceitful and desperately wicked hearts of ours we reproduce today Peter's history.

Yes, I will be very bold to say we can parallel Peter's history by our own. *We have* known something—most of us, at any rate—of the bliss that filled Peter's soul upon the Mount, and of the brave enthusiasm that fired his heart at Caesarea. Yes, we have had our days when we were fellow citizens of the saints and of the household of God. But if we have shared Peter's bliss, we have also shared his sin and blame. We have forsaken our Lord as Peter did, and we have denied Him before men as he did. Yes, there have been days in our experience when we have sinned so grievously and desperately as almost to be beyond forgiveness. The human heart is the best confirmation of Peter's history. Heaven and hell contended for the mastery in Peter's heart long ago; heaven and hell are contending for the mastery in our divided and distracted souls today.

The Evolution of Peter

"Thou art Simon, the son of John," said Jesus, when He first set eyes upon this man who was to become the chief of the Apostles. "Thou art Simon, thou shalt be called Cephas," which is by interpretation Peter—that is, "a rock." If I had to search the New Testament through I could not discover a more beautiful illustration of the charity and hopefulness of our blessed Lord than I find in these His first words to Peter. For when Simon came to Him that day he was anything but a "rock" man. He was a man of sand that day, and for many a day after that. It took months, it took years, it took a lifetime to turn Simon into Peter—the man of sand into the man of rock.

"In a gallery in Europe," says Dr. Miller in his little book on the *Friendship of Jesus,* "there hang side by side Rembrandt's first picture, a simple sketch, imperfect and faulty, and his great masterpiece which all men admire. And so in the two names, Simon and Peter, we have first the rude fisherman, the man as he was before Jesus began His work on him, and, second, the man as he became after the friendship of Jesus and the teaching of Jesus and the discipline of life had wrought their transformations in him."

"Thou shalt be called the Rock," said Jesus about this man when he was brought to Him at the first by Andrew his brother. With the love that hopes all things our Lord hoped and believed and prophesied that Simon would become a man of rock-like steadfastness, as unmoved by the wrath and spite of men as the black bastions that line our coasts are by the waves that fret and foam at their feet. But for long it seemed as if Christ's prophecy and hope would be disappointed. For Simon in the Gospels is a weak and vacillating creature.

It is the man of sand you see in the man who ran away in the garden and who denied Christ with oaths and curses in the Judgment Hall at the taunt of a serving maid. Yet Christ did not lose heart or hope for His fallen disciple. "Thou shalt be called Peter," He said again to his penitent and well-nigh despairing soul, and in a few weeks you find that same man who fled in the garden speaking boldly in the name of the Lord Jesus in the streets of Jerusalem, and witnessing courageously for Him before governors and kings.

Yes, he is the man of sand all through the Gospels; but in the Book of the Acts, on the day of Pentecost, at the gate of the Temple called Beautiful, before the Sanhedrim—he is Peter the Rock. Yet I will not say that Simon never turned coward after Pentecost, that he was always a man of rock after Pentecost. To the end of life he was always contending with the weakness and cowardice of his own heart, and more than once he fell as he did in the Judgment Hall. Once in Antioch, for fear of some Jews from Jerusalem, he withdrew like a coward from the fellowship of the Gentile Christians, and so stirred Paul's righteous soul to burning indignation and provoked from him a public rebuke.

And again, if the tradition be true, toward the end of his life he turned coward at Rome. It was the time of the fierce and terrible Neronic persecutions. Christians were being put to death in awful and unheard-of ways. Peter's soul, as he heard of Christians serving as lighted torches in Nero's gardens, and dying hideous deaths in Roman amphitheatres, felt his heart faint within him. To escape death he fled from Rome. But as he hurried along the Appian way, about two miles from the gates, he was met by the Savior traveling toward the city. Struck with amazement, Peter cried, *"Domine, quo vadis?"* ("Lord, whither goest Thou?") And the Savior, looking upon him as

He had looked upon him long before in the Judgment Hall, said, "I go to Rome to be crucified a second time."

It was Peter's last failure. It was the last trace of the sand in his nature. He was Peter the Rock from that day to the end. With head erect and proud step, he returned to Rome to witness bravely for Christ until such day as in the barrack square he hung head downwards on a cross for his Lord's dear sake. When I think of Peter's history, of his many and shameful falls and his final victory, two truths come home to my soul with mighty power:

The Forgiving Grace of Christ

First, from Simon Peter's history *a new and subduing idea of the forgiving grace of Christ comes to me.* "Lord," Simon had said to Jesus one day, "how oft shall my brother sin against me and I forgive him? Till seven times?" It was well for Simon that his thoughts on forgiveness were not his Master's. Had Jesus accepted Simon's notions about the limits of forgiveness Simon would never have reached the pearly gates, he would never have entered the inheritance of the saints in light; he would never have worn the crown and the robe of righteousness. Had Jesus adopted Simon's limits of forgiveness, then Simon himself would have been today in the outer darkness, where there is weeping and wailing and gnashing of teeth.

"I say not unto thee until seven times," was our Lord's reply, "but until seventy times seven." Simon needed the seventy times seven for he sinned and sinned and sinned again. He fell and fell and fell again. Simon himself is an illustration of grace that never wearies of forgiving. Yes, Simon is a monument of the patient and pardoning love of Christ. I have fancied that many a time Peter said to his soul, anticipating the words of our own Gospel poet: "O to grace how great a debtor, daily I'm constrained to be." Again and again I am persuaded he used to take himself as a text and preach a sermon of comfort and hope to downcast and despairing souls.

When he came to die it was a saying of his beloved brother Paul that he wished to have graven on his tombstone, and that was this: "Where sin abounded, grace did much more abound." With Peter as my text I would preach that same comforting sermon he used to preach long ago. Yes, I know we have sinned grievously and sinned often, but Jesus forgives even unto seventy times seven. I say, even unto seventy times seven. Friends may cast you off, parents may disown you, all who know you may despair of you, but there is mercy with Jesus Christ. O men and women laden with iniquities sinning and sinning and sinning again, I know of One who has not despaired of you. I know of One whose patience has not failed. Come to Peter's Savior, and you shall find that—

> *"Unwearied in forgiveness still,*
> *His heart can only love."*

The Restoring Power of Christ

A *second* thing I learn from Peter's story, I get a *new idea of the restoring power of Christ.* "Thou shalt be called Peter—a Rock," said Jesus. To turn Simon—the unstable, unreliable, vacillating Simon—into a rock! What a work that was! But the power of Christ accomplished it, so that the man who cursed at the taunt of a serving maid without a tremor faced a hideous death at Rome.

With Peter as my text I am prepared to preach this glorious Gospel: There is not a person, however wicked and broken and helpless, that Jesus cannot by His Almighty power restore. "Thou shalt become a rock," Christ says to you and me—brave, strong, steadfast, immovable. To you, young person, frightened of your associates in the gang, Christ says, "Thou shalt become a rock"—absolutely unshaken by their taunts or sneers or laughter. To you the victim of sin, hating it and doing it, loathing it and returning to it, and half inclined to abandon the struggle as hopeless, Christ says, "Thou shalt become a rock," against which temptation shall break in vain. To you the person of weak will and irresolute purpose, Christ says, "Thou shalt become a rock," steadfast, immovable, always abounding in the work of the Lord.

Yes, with Peter as my text, I preach the restorability of the weakest and most despairing. The hand that made out of Simon a rock man; the hand that made out of John and Mark a witness and faithful martyr; the hand that made out of a power-mad politician the greatest prison worker of modern times, can take us—weak, timid, broken as we are—and make us pillars in the Temple of our God from which we shall no more go out.

Peter's Pride

I have left myself but a page or two to look at Peter's chief fault and his chief virtue. His chief fault was his *pride*, his *boastful* and *braggart self-confidence*. I am not trying to utter a paradox, but simply stating literal truth when I say that the very energy and force and masterfulness of Peter's nature, which constituted him the leader of the twelve, was also the direct and immediate cause of his bitterest humiliations and failures.

The secret of victorious strength in the Christian life is self-distrust. "When I am weak," so the Apostle Paul puts it in a sentence, "then am I strong." When a man realizes his weakness, he casts himself upon God, and then he is able to overcome the principalities and powers and spiritual hosts of wickedness which are drawn up to do battle against his soul. That was a secret Peter did not learn for many a day. There were certain words of our Lord, such as, "Apart from Me ye can do nothing," which, as far as Peter was concerned, fell on absolutely deaf ears. This strong, forceful, masterful man had complete and perfect confidence in himself. "Though all men should be offended in Thee, I will never be offended," he boasted.

"Simon, Simon," said our Lord to him in solemn warning, "behold, Satan hath desired to have you, that he may sift you as wheat, but I made supplication for thee, that thy faith fail not quite."

Peter was hurt, almost insulted, by his Master's warning words. "Lord," he replied proudly, "with Thee I am ready to go to prison and to death." And before that night had passed this proud, self-reliant, self-confident man had denied his Lord three times. Yes, Peter's very strength was his weakness, and at the last it was the discovery of his weakness that made him strong. Peter fell through his pride, through his over-weening self-confidence, and there is one verse in his first letter which seems to me to be addressed specially to strong and self-reliant men. It is written in the Apostle's life blood. It is this: "Be sober, be watchful; for your adversary the devil, as a roaring lion, walketh about, seeking whom he may devour."

Peter's Love

On the other hand, Peter's chief virtue, his saving grace, *was his love.* Peter loved the Lord with all the strength of his eager, impetu-

ous, enthusiastic heart. It was love that made him leave all and follow
Him at the first. It was love—mistaken love, but still love—that
would have saved Christ from the Via Dolorosa. It was love that
made him say at the Supper, in his own impulsive way, "Thou shalt
never wash my feet"; and then, when he knew what the act signified,
"Not my feet only, but also my hands and my head."

It was love that made his sword leap out of its scabbard in the
garden. It was love that made him follow his Lord into the Judgment
Hall. It was love that sent him out after the denial to weep bitterly.

Yes, whatever charges may be brought against Peter, this at any
rate may be said in his favor: he loved his Lord with a deep, passionate, enthusiastic love. Pick me out the most rapturous phrases from
the Book of Psalms, from the Song of Songs, from the letters of
Samuel Rutherford or the writings of any other spiritual writer, and I
will say that they are all true of Peter. When he gave his heart Peter
gave it utterly and altogether: "Whom have I in heaven but Thee,
and there is none on earth that I desire beside Thee."

Turn to the last chapter of John and read that moving story of the
conversation between Jesus and His erring disciple by the lake. "Lovest
thou Me?" asked Jesus—once, twice, thrice—as if it were the one and
only vital question. "Yea, Lord, Thou knowest that I love Thee,"
answered Peter. "Lord, Thou knowest all things, Thou knowest this
deceitful and wicked heart of mine, *Thou knowest that I love Thee.*"

"Love," says Peter in his first Epistle, "covereth a multitude of
sins." It covered the sleep, and the forsaking and the denial. Christ
had no eyes for them; He had eyes for nothing but for His disciple's
passionate and burning love.

Love still covers a multitude of sins. "Her sins," said Christ of the
woman who bathed His feet, "her sins, which are many, are forgiven,
for she loved much." And it matters not how grievously and how
often we may have sinned, they will all be forgotten and forgiven as
Peter's were, as that woman's were, if only we love as Peter and that
woman did.

"And I will give thee the keys of the kingdom of heaven," said
Christ to Peter. And if you believe me, He is willing to give that
same key to us. For the key is "Love." Heaven is closed against
learning. Heaven is closed against rank. Heaven is closed against
wealth. But heaven is open to "love." The gates of the city opened
wide to receive this man who, whatever his faults and failings and

sins, could yet look his Lord in the face and say, "Lord, Thou knowest all things, Thou knowest that I love Thee!" Let me ask you this plain and simple question. Do you love the Lord Jesus Christ? Are you altogether and entirely in love with Him? Do you love Him better than health, better than wealth, better than fame, better than home, better than your nearest and your best? Is your heart utterly and absolutely set upon Jesus Christ? Can you challenge Him as Peter did, and say, "Lord, Thou knowest all things, *Thou knowest* that I love Thee"? Can you say that? Look into your hearts and tell me, can you say that? Then blessed are you, for you have the key to the kingdom of heaven; and when you leave this earth the massive gates of the city will open to welcome you and all the trumpets shall sound for you on the other side.

3

JAMES

"James the son of Zebedee, and his brother John; (to them he gave the name, Boanerges, which means, Sons of Thunder)."
—Mark 3:17 NIV

IN MY DISCUSSION of Simon Peter I referred to the fact that the Evangelists, while unanimous as to which of the Apostles should be mentioned first, differ as to which of the glorious company should be mentioned second. In the lists of Matthew and Luke, coupled with the name of Simon Peter, the primary of the twelve, I find the name of Andrew, Simon Peter's brother. But in Mark's list, next to the name of Simon Peter, I find the name of James, the son of Zebedee.

Had I nothing but the lists supplied by the Evangelists to guide me, I should be in doubt as to which of the Apostles really ranked second in the blessed and glorious company. But my doubt is at once dispelled when I begin to peruse the Gospel history. When I refer to the Gospels, this is what I find: just as our Lord called twelve out of the multitude of the disciples that they might be with Him, so out of the twelve He chose three for a closer and still more special intimacy. The Prime Minister of Great Britain has his Cabinet of fifteen or twenty persons with whom from time to time he takes counsel on great affairs of State. But within the Cabinet there is a committee of the Cabinet consisting of four or five of its most influential members, whom the Prime Minister admits to a still more intimate confidence.

In exactly the same way there was an inner circle within the circle of the Apostolate, and that inner circle consisted of Peter, James and

John. These three men enjoyed a special intimacy with Christ, standing in closer relationship to Him than the rest. They shared His confidences and were permitted to be near Him on some of the great experiences of His life.

When Jesus entered Jairus's house to have His first wrestle with death, He allowed no man to follow with Him save Peter, James, and John the brother of James. When He ascended the Mount to talk with Moses and Elijah concerning the exodus which He was about to accomplish in Jerusalem, He took with Him as the sole witnesses of that never-to-be-forgotten scene these same favored three—Peter, James and John. And when again, on the night of His betrayal, He agonized beneath the crushing load of human sin in the garden, it was Peter, James and John He called to be the sharers of His bitter sorrow, as before on the Mount He had called them to behold His glory.

Yes, with the Gospels before me I have no doubt at all that next in importance and influence to Peter came not Andrew his brother, but James and John, the sons of Zebedee. John, the author of the Apocalypse and the Epistles and that incomparable fourth Gospel, was, as those books of his abundantly testify, a man of soaring vision and seraphic spirit, one of the greatest spiritual geniuses the world has ever known. Yet I will make bold to say that in the days of our Lord's earthly sojourn—yes, and until the day James drank of his Lord's cup and was baptized with his Lord's baptism—the younger brother was overshadowed by the elder, and it was James, not John, who, next to Peter, was counted as the chief pillar of the Church. I say this for two reasons: *First*, because John, with one exception, is always mentioned last of the great three (Peter, James and John, such is the order), and is invariably described in the Gospels as the brother of James, just as Andrew is described as the brother of Simon Peter, James being apparently the better known and more prominent of the two. *Secondly* and conclusively, please note that when some fourteen years after the death of Christ, Herod Agrippa sought to vex and harass and destroy the Church, he did so by singling out its two most influential and energetic leaders for death. Those two leaders, as we find from the twelfth chapter of Acts, were Peter and James. With the Gospels and the Book of Acts before me, I will venture to assert that, next to Peter, there was amongst the twelve none greater than James the son of Zebedee and Salome, and the cousin of our Lord.

James in Scripture

About this man, who was a chief among the Apostles and a very pillar of the Church, Scripture tells us very little. James, indeed, can only be said to figure in two incidents in the Gospels, and even in those he is associated with his brother John. If little is said of James during the days of our Lord's life, less still is said of him in the days that followed the Resurrection. He lived for some fourteen years after that great and notable event; but you will search the Book of the Acts of the Apostles in vain for any record of any word James ever said or any deed he ever did. The Book never mentions James, never refers to James, never speaks of James, until in chapter twelve it makes room for this brief but pathetic notice: "And Herod killed James the brother of John with a sword." Thus, only half-a-dozen sentences tell us all we will ever know about James. Yet I repeat again that amongst the twelve—with the solitary exception of Peter— there was none greater than Zebedee's eldest son. Which leads me to point out that fame is not always the true measure of greatness, and that a man's reputation here is no index to his station in heaven. Reputation is what most men seek after. They do their deeds, like the Pharisees of old, to be seen and heard of men. They love to be talked about and praised. But James did his work and cared nothing for reputation. There had been a time when he was eager to be first, but he had long ceased to care about station or position so long as he could do his Lord's work. Yes, James in course of years became one of those of whom Lowell speaks—

> *The bravely dumb who did their deed,*
> *And scorned to blot it with a name;*
> *Men of the plain heroic breed,*
> *Who loved Heaven's silence more than fame.*

Had he known that half-a-dozen sentences would be all the record of his brave and faithful life that would descend to posterity, it would have caused him no distress.

But men come to their own in time. Many a man of great reputation on earth has had with shame to take the lowest room in heaven, while James, whose record is contained in six sentences, sits today on the throne nearest to his Lord. And with the vision of James upon his

throne before my eyes, I would repeat the Lord's solemn word once
again: "There are last that shall be first, and there are first that shall
be last."

James' Zeal

The total record of James in the New Testament does not extend
to more than some half-dozen sentences—and yet so illuminating are
those sentences that in them James' character stands fully revealed.
"And them," says Mark, in his account of the call of James and John
to the Apostolate, "and them Jesus surnamed Boanerges, which is
Sons of Thunder." In that single sentence you have the key to James'
character. Yes, if we had nothing but that name Boanerges we should
feel we knew James through and through. All the other references to
James are but amplifications and illustrations of this surname which
Jesus gave him.

James was a "Son of Thunder." What does that mean? It means a
man of stormy and tempestuous zeal—not a man of eloquence, as
some commentators say, still less a man of sonorous voice, as Dr.
Morison would have us believe—it means a man of fiery and enthusiastic, almost turbulent, zeal.

Zeal was James' chief and salient characteristic. He was the most
earnest and fiery spirit in the Apostolic company. There were others
of the holy twelve who had become conspicuous for other and different qualities. Peter was known for his ready speech; John was known
for his mystical contemplativeness; Philip was known for his practical
common-sense; Andrew was known for his missionary activity; Thomas was known for his philosophical mind. But for zeal, flaming,
enthusiastic, almost irrepressible zeal, there was none to compare
with James, Zebedee's eldest son. That flaming, enthusiastic zeal of
his carried him to the second place among the Apostles, and to his
seat upon the heavenly throne.

"It is good," writes the Apostle Paul to the Galatians, "to be zealously affected always in a good thing." Now James was zealously
affected in the cause of Jesus Christ. We do not know how or when
James first became acquainted with Jesus, nor do we know how or
when his passionate love for Jesus was first kindled within his heart.
But this we know—James was so zealous for Jesus Christ that, without a moment's hesitation, he sacrificed everything for His sake.

In the first chapter of the Gospel of Mark the following account of James' call is written: "And when he had gone a little farther He saw James the son of Zebedee and John his brother, who also were in the ship mending their nets. And straightway He called them, and they left their father Zebedee in the ship with the hired servants and went after Him."

"Lo," said Peter in later days, "we have left all and have followed Thee." Everyone of the twelve had left all, but none had left so much as James and John. For, according to the Gospels, James and John seem to have been drawn from a higher social circle than the rest of the twelve. Their father was a prosperous man of business, having servants under him. Their family had connections with some of the leading families in Jerusalem.

James and John had more to give up than the rest when *they* followed Christ: Peter and Andrew left their boats and nets, but James and John had to leave father and mother as well. Matthew had to leave the odious tollbooth, but James and John had to leave a happy and comfortable home. None of these things weighed with them. They left father and mother for the Gospel's sake. They gladly suffered the loss of home and comfort and social station, and counted them without value that they might win Christ and be found in Him, not having a righteousness of their own, but the righteousness which is of God by faith. That same zeal for Christ which made James along with his brother leave all and follow Christ at the first, flamed in his heart to the very end, and sent him at last to lay down his life in his dear Lord's cause. Yes, zeal—fiery, enthusiastic, passionate zeal—was James' leading and most striking characteristic.

But this earnest and zealous man had his grave faults—faults born almost out of his virtue; and these faults were (1) intolerance, and (2) ambition.

James' Intolerance

Zeal is a high and beautiful Christian virtue, but zeal itself, ungoverned and misdirected, may become a vice. Some of the most terrible deeds in human history have been done through mistaken religious zeal. "I bear them witness," says Paul of his fellow-countrymen, the Jews, in his letter to the Romans, "that they have a zeal for God, *but not according to knowledge.*" Paul might have quoted himself in his

early days as a conspicuous example of that ignorant and misguided
zeal. He could not remember the time when he had not been zealous
for God; but all the years prior to the great light that flashed upon
him on the way to Damascus, it had been a zeal *not according to
knowledge.* For this is what the blind zeal of those early days had
driven him to do—it had made him raise his voice against Stephen,
and then stand by consenting unto his death. It had made him rage
furiously and become exceedingly angry against the Christians, so
that he went everywhere arresting men and women and casting them
into prison. "For zeal, persecuting the Church."

In much the same way the zeal of James was in the early days of his
Apostleship a zeal *not according to knowledge.* It happened one day,
toward the end of our Lord's life, that He passed through Samaria on
His way to Jerusalem and the Cross. He sent messengers before Him, to
a certain village of the Samaritans that lay in His path, to make ready
for Him. But the people would not receive Him. With insulting and
bitter words they refused to give Him hospitality because His face was
as though He were going to Jerusalem. They bade Him—a Jew—go
and seek entertainment of His own countrymen the Jews. And with
that the "Sons of Thunder" were all aflame, and in their zeal for the
honor of their Lord they would have wiped out those rude and surly
Samaritans from off the face of the earth. "Wilt Thou," said they, "that
we bid fire to come down from heaven and consume them?"

Flaming zeal easily becomes intolerant, and the zealot quickly de-
velops into a persecutor. John and James would have called for the
fires of the pit if they had had their own way in that little Samaritan
village. In that cry of theirs breathes the very spirit of the men who in
the name of religion burned John Huss in Constance, gibbetted Savonarola in Florence, consigned Hooper, Ridley and Latimer to the flames
in England, and roasted old women to death in Salem, Massachu-
setts.

But the Lord rebuked these would-be persecutors with a stern and
scathing rebuke. They had shown that they were of quite another
spirit from Him who came not to kill but to keep, not to destroy
men's lives but to save them.

For this persecuting fury that filled the hearts of James and his
brother that day I have no word of excuse or apology. It was altogether hateful and un-Christian. And yet in their fierce intolerance there
is a touch of nobleness. At any rate, I will say this: I had rather James

and John flame out into wrath as they did, than that they should have been able to witness insult done to their Lord without a quiver or a pang. There is something worse than intolerant zeal, and that is Laodicean indifference. And that worse thing has come upon many of us today. It seems that no one becomes wrathful and indignant nowadays. We care for Christ so little that we can bear to hear Him insulted and maligned without being angry. Yes, nominal Christians in these perverse and crooked days are able to sit still and smile when Christ is made the subject of the gibes of wicked fools.

In the conversation of society, speech which is dishonoring to Christ is all too common. Who is there here that has ever risen in sacred wrath to protest against it? Who has been brave enough to stand for Christ as did Stephen so long ago? Who is there here that has dared to rise and confess before unbelieving men, "I am Christ's servant still"? On the other hand, who is not conscious that he has often been silent when he ought to have spoken, often been dumb when he ought to have made protest?

I confess to you I had rather stand at the Judgment with these two brothers, James and John, aflame with terrible and ruthless zeal for the honor of Christ, than I would with those who can see Christ mocked and buffeted and spat upon, and smile through it all.

There is hope for the zealot, for the man of burning and flaming soul; there is little or none for the man of such tepid love that he can see his Lord insulted without indignation or pain. Listen to this woe addressed to Laodicea, but applicable to these limp and placid days of ours: "I know thy works; that thou art neither cold nor hot. I would thou wert cold or hot. So then, because thou art lukewarm and neither cold nor hot, I will spew thee out of my mouth."

James' Ambition

James' second fault was his *ambition*. "The greatest zealots," as Dr. A. B. Bruce says, "were also the most ambitious, a circumstance that will not surprise the student of human nature." James and his brother, proudly conscious of their great zeal in the service of Christ, thought that for their zeal they had a claim to the first places in the affections and the kingdom of Christ.

But a rude shock had been given to their hopes by that great word Christ spoke to Peter at Caesarea Philippi. When our Lord said to

Peter, "Thou art Peter, and on this rock I will build my Church," James and John turned well-nigh sick with envy. Yes, they turned pale and green with envy. King Saul became so jealous of the young warrior, David, that he eventually reached the point of suicide. Thus it is with envy.

Plutarch says of Themistocles that so ambitious was he to stand first in the esteem of the people of Athens, that after the battle of Marathon, when the people could talk of nothing but the bravery and skill of Miltiades the victorious general, he would spend hours in solitude so as to avoid hearing the praises of his rival sung.

"Yea," says Plutarch, "he got no rest day nor night, neither would he frequent festivals, nor keep company with his friends. And when asked what was the matter with him and what he ailed, this was his reply: 'Miltiades' victory would not let him sleep.'"

Just so our Lord's commendation of Peter would not let James and his brother sleep. Waking and sleeping they could never forget that word. They coveted the first place for themselves, and could not bear the thought that Peter should be advanced above them. From that day forward James and John never ceased to plot and scheme for their own advancement, and in the tenth chapter of Mark you can read of the ugly episode in which their plotting culminated.

To help their plan they had dragged their mother into the conspiracy under the fond delusion that Jesus could deny nothing to his mother's sister. So one day Salome, with her two sons, came and flung herself at the feet of Christ in the attitude of worship. "We would," said this shameless trio, "that Thou shouldest do for us whatsoever we desire."

"What would ye that I should do for you?" asks Jesus.

"Grant unto us that we may sit one on Thy right hand and the other on Thy left hand in Thy glory," is their answer. And with that answer they laid their envious and jealous hearts bare to their Master's gaze.

Peter was all the trouble; Peter's primacy would not let them sleep! What a terrible thing is envy! And how cruel it is—cruel as the grave. And how it creeps, like some foul poison, everywhere. Here in the Apostolate, in the inner circle of three, are two pining with envy of the third.

I have no adjectives for the James and John we meet in Mark 10. Their request was ignorant, presumptuous, irreverent, and intensely selfish, says Dr. Bruce, Yes, it was all that and more; and if the narrative ended at verse thirty-seven I should have despaired of James and John. But when I read on I find hints of the nobleness of these brothers even in the narrative that most terribly reveals their faults.

"Ye know not what ye ask," says Jesus. "Are ye able to drink the cup that I drink, or to be baptized with the baptism that I am baptized with?"

And they said unto Him, "We are able."

That was a searching question Christ put to them. "Are ye able to drink the cup that I drink of?" They wanted thrones—Christ asks them can they drink His bitter cup? They wanted a crown—Christ asks them can they bear His Cross? These men, looking into their own hearts and knowing that their zeal and passion for Christ was the deepest thing in their souls, answer humbly and yet boldly, "We are able."

What is this answer? Is it a bit of inconsiderate and foolish boasting? No, this is love's daring. "We are able." It is a great answer, a moving answer, a most magnificent answer. If they were cravens and cowards in their request, they are mighty men of valor in their confession. "We are able." If they wanted thrones, they were ready to pay the price for them.

There are some who want the throne without the cup and the baptism; there are some who want the crown without the Cross; there are some who want the white robe without the great tribulation. But James was willing to pay the price. Like Ignatius, that eager martyr, he was ready to cry, "Come fire and iron and grapplings with wild beasts, cuttings and manglings, wrenching of bones, hacking of limbs, crushings of my whole body; come cruel tortures of the devil to assail me—only be it mine to attain unto Jesus Christ."

Like Francis Xavier, that flaming missionary and evangelist, he was ready to cry out for "men to suffer for his Lord," and to say, like him, "Whatever be the form of torture or of death that awaits me, I am ready to suffer it ten thousand times for my Lord's sake." Yes, James looked into his own heart and then into his Lord's face, and felt he could drink any cup of sorrow and bear any baptism of pain for his Lord's sake. So he answered with simple and sublime confidence, *"We are able."*

This was no empty and unconsidered boast as history plainly proves. The Gospels and the Book of Acts do not tell us very much about

James. But I can with perfect safety supply the omission to the extent of saying that while James' spirit became more enlightened, so that he lost his intolerance and ambition, he lost none of his zeal. Of all the Christian preachers there was none who preached with such vehemence and passion and zeal as James. He never grew tired in that blessed work. In season and out, he was at it and none were able to resist the power and grace with which he spoke.

So it came to pass that when Herod Agrippa resolved to destroy the Church, his counselors told him that the first man to be seized must be James the son of Zebedee. The Christians, hearing the first mutterings of the storm, tried to persuade James to flee. But flight was not in his bold and eager nature. As the danger drew nearer, he preached the more vehemently, and cried out to the people with tears to be reconciled to God. And then the blow fell. "And Herod killed James the brother of John with the sword."

On that day James drank his Lord's cup and was baptized with the Lord's baptism, and on that very same day James took his seat upon the throne at his Lord's right hand.

Let me ask you a question. You all want to gain the throne. There is no one who does not hope and expect to win the throne at last. Are you able to drink your Lord's cup and to be baptized with your Lord's baptism? For the cup and the baptism are the conditions of the throne. Can you drink your Lord's cup of sorrow? Are you able to face scorn, hatred, insult, persecution, death, for your Lord? Can you answer with James to those questions, "We are able"? Then happy are you! For if you suffer with Christ, you shall also be glorified together.

There is an old legend which says that one of those who bore false witness against James before Herod was so overcome by the Apostle's earnestness and zeal and holy courage, that he then and there confessed himself a Christian. He was immediately carried off with him to execution. On the way to the block he craved forgiveness of the Apostle, and the Apostle gave him a kiss, and said, "Pax vobis!" and so James and his latest convert died together. Had we but James' spirit, his earnestness, his passion, his enthusiasm, we should be able in like manner to overthrow and convert those who oppose us. We are crippled by our coldness, paralyzed by our lack of zeal. We lack earnestness, devotion, passion, fire. And I know of no more appropriate and suitable prayer for us than this—

"Come, Holy Spirit, heavenly Dove,
    With all Thy quickening powers,
Kindle a flame of sacred love
    In these cold hearts of ours.

"Dear Lord and shall we ever lie
    At this poor dying rate,
Our love so faint, so cold to Thee,
    And Thine to us so great.

"Come, Holy Spirit, heavenly Dove,
    With all Thy quickening powers,
Come shed abroad the Savior's love,
    And that shall kindle ours."

4

JOHN

"The disciple whom Jesus loved."   —John 21:20

THE GOSPEL NARRATIVE makes it quite clear that just as out of the whole multitude of His disciples Christ chose twelve to be with Him, so again out of the twelve He chose three for a closer and still more special intimacy. Within the circle of the Apostles there was an inner circle of three disciples who stood in closer relationship to Christ than the rest, who were permitted to share in the supreme experiences of His life, who entered with Him into the death chamber in Jairus' house, who beheld His glory on the Holy Mount, and who witnessed His agony in the garden of this inner circle.

Peter the son of John was the first, and James the son of Zebedee was the second, and the third was John the brother of James. Now, judging from the order in which the names of these three are mentioned in the Gospels, I should gather that John was more or less overshadowed by James and Peter, and that he did not occupy as prominent a place or as influential a position in the Apostolic College as they did. John was a man of quiet, contemplative, almost mystical spirit. He was not the equal of Peter or his own brother James in practical energy and gifts of leadership, the consequence being that, as compared with them, he occupied a subordinate position among the twelve. And yet, if I had my choice today, I would rather be John than either James or Peter. Yes, I covet John's place more than I do Peter's primacy or James' exalted throne. Peter and James were first *among the twelve,* but John was first *in the affections of his Lord!*

Peter and James occupied the chief places in the *Apostolic College*, but John occupied the chief place *in the heart of Christ*. There is something better to be said of John than that he was the Primate of the Apostles; there is something better to be said of John than that he was a prince and ruler among the early believers. This better thing, this blessed and most beautiful thing, is to be said of John—he was "the disciple whom Jesus loved."

The Testimony to John's Character

I can conceive of no more magnificent testimony to John's character than is contained in the phrase of my text. Indeed, I will be bold to say that more splendid tribute has never been paid to any man, from the beginning of time even until now, than is paid to John in the sentence of my text. Great words have been spoken and written of some of the eminent saints of ancient days in the pages of the Old Testament. Of Enoch, for instance, it is said that "he walked with God." Of Moses it is said that "he talked with God as friend with friend." Of David it is said that "he was a man after God's own heart." But here is a greater word still.

Of John the son of Zebedee it is said that he was the disciple *whom Jesus loved*. There was something in John so gracious, so winsome, so heavenly, that Jesus—shall I say it?—fell in love with him, and the soul of Jesus was knit unto the soul of John, and He loved him as His own soul. And I say again, finer testimony to John's character I could not conceive. For by this token I know that this same John was the most saintly and Christ-like of the Apostles.

Yes, select Peter for practical energy, James for zeal, Andrew for missionary activity, Bartholomew for simple faith; but for a pure and Christ-like soul, turn to John the son of Zebedee. We keep company with those with whom we are spiritually akin. Jesus found His kindred soul in John. Yes, He who did no sin, neither was guile found in His mouth, found in John the soul most like His own; so Jesus kept company with John. In John's companionship, Jesus took great and deep delight. And I want no further testimony to John's character than this. Jesus delighted in John, He kept company with John, He gave a special place in His heart to John—John was the disciple whom Jesus loved.

That, I believe, was John's great glory and boast. Other things—

great and splendid things—might have been said of John. He had a *mind*. He has been called the Christian Plato. "John, fisherman's son and all," says Dr. Alexander Whyte, "was born with one of the finest minds that have ever been bestowed by God's goodness upon any of the sons of men." The eagle, the king of birds, is John's symbol in act, and finer symbol could not be—for a more piercing and soaring mind than John's the world has never known. Read the first fourteen verses of his glorious Gospel, and you will know that John had a mind that could scale the loftiest height, and sound the lowest depths.

He had a *pen* also, so that this unknown Galilean has become one of the Immortals of the world. The fourth Gospel, the Apocalypse and the Epistles—amongst the Divinest books in the world—came from John's pen. And on the strength of the fourteenth chapter of the Gospel, and the fourth chapter in his first Epistle, and those glowing, dazzling twenty-first and twenty-second chapters of the Apocalypse, I will assert and maintain John's claim to be one of the great writers of the world.

And yet, it was not on his mind or his pen that John boasted himself. It was not on his matchless books that John prided himself. Mind and pen, books and fame—John counted them but as the small dust of the balance. They were but dross to John. The one thing on which he prided himself, the one thing in which he gloried and boasted himself was this—that he was beloved of Jesus Christ. "God forbid," he would say when men talked to him of his influence and fame, "God forbid that I should glory save in this—that Jesus loved even me."

And here, my reader, I am tempted to break away from John for a moment to ask you a plain, straightforward question: What, is it in which you boast and pride yourselves the most? What at this present moment, do you consider your chief glory? I look abroad, and I see men priding themselves upon diverse things. Some pride themselves on their birth and ancient lineage; some pride themselves upon their social station; some pride themselves upon their wealth. Some pride themselves upon their power; some pride themselves upon their intellectual attainments and their fame. But on what do *you* pride yourself?

If you were asked honestly to say what it is in which you take most delight, what would you answer? I have put these questions to my own heart; yes, I have proved and searched my own heart with them. And I will be frank to say I found a certain lust of fame in my heart. I found a certain pride of reputation there. I found a certain glorying in the power my pulpit gives me in my heart. But if you asked me what I count my chiefest possession, I answer fame and reputation and power are nothing to the love of Christ. Yes, this is my boast, my glory, my pride, that I, a sin-stained and guilt-laden man, can yet say with humble but joyful confidence, "The Son of God loved *me* and gave Himself for *me.*"

In what do you boast and glory yourselves? What do *you* count your greatest possession? "Forefancy your dying bed," as saintly old Rutherford says, for it is only in the white light of eternity that things assume their right proportions. "Forefancy your dying bed!" Imagine yourselves upon it before it comes! In that solemn hour, of what will you boast yourselves? Of fame? No. Of wealth? No. Of station? No. Of high lineage? No. This only will a man care to boast about when his last hour comes—that Christ loves him, a poor sinner. Boast in that amazing and stupendous fact that Christ loves *you.*

In order that you may have it to boast of when your end comes, ask God to emancipate you so wholly, so entirely, so absolutely from the fascination and vain glories of the world, that, like John, your one delight will be in the love of Christ, and like our own Evangelical poet you shall sing:

> *"Forbid it, Lord, that I should boast,*
> *Save in the Cross of Christ my God;*
> *All the vain things that charm me most,*
> *I sacrifice them to His blood."*

The Natural John

"The disciple whom Jesus loved." Such was John. And yet sometimes when I read the Gospels I am tempted to wonder that Jesus loved John at all. I could take John and make him a text for a sermon on the wideness and generosity of the love of Jesus Christ. Yes, with John as my text I could preach the blessed truth of love for all, in spite of imperfections and sins. "Just as I am," we say in our old familiar hymn, "Thou wilt receive, wilt welcome, pardon, cleanse, relieve." And for proof of that I would quote the fact that Jesus lavished His love upon John; for John, the natural John, the aboriginal John, was in many respects of a spirit wholly alien and contrary to the spirit of Christ.

To John, as to James, Christ gave the surname Boanerges. Like his brother, he was a man of thunder—a man of fierce, vehement temper. Read the story of how John, ablaze with anger, called down fire from heaven on the Samaritans. Do you wonder that this should be the man whom Jesus loved? Read the story of his selfish request of the highest throne, and are you not surprised that this should be the man whom Jesus loved? Read that other story of how John rebuked the man who was casting out devils, and forbade Him continuing His blessed work. Do you not marvel that this should be the man whom Jesus loved? I say again, I cannot read of this intolerant, hot-tempered, selfishly ambitious man without wondering sometimes that Jesus ever loved him at all.

How was it Jesus came to love John? His faults would have irritated me, they would have angered me. How was it that in spite of them John was the disciple whom Jesus loved?

The Redeeming Grace in John

Well, here we come across one of the most beautiful characteristics of our Lord. His judgments of men were always kindly. He always saw what was best in them. He had a quick eye for any virtue or grace. "He knew," says John himself, "what was in man." He did not judge a man by his only too manifest faults and failings; He looked into his heart, and judged him by what He saw there. If Jesus saw any promise of future goodness in a man's soul, He judged him not by what he was, but by what he might become.

"He could," as Dr. Bruce says, "regard with complacency even some grapes in their season, for the sake of the goodly fruit into which they should ripen." He saw, for instance, the desire for a new life that filled Zacchaeus' heart; and so, while everyone else called him a cheating publican, Jesus spoke of him as a "Son of Abraham." He saw the penitence and yearning for purity that filled the heart of the woman who was a sinner, and so, while others flung at her the coarse and brutal name of "harlot," Jesus called her "daughter." Beneath John's impatience and bad temper and intolerance and selfish ambition, Jesus saw something which gave promise of saintliness in later days, and that something was John's *passionate devotion to Himself*. And Jesus loved him for that.

That John did love Jesus with all the ardor of his soul is written large on the pages of the Gospel history. John was one of the first two disciples Jesus ever had, and from that memorable day when, at the bidding of John the Baptist, he had followed Jesus, to the day when as an old man he gave up the ghost, Jesus filled and absorbed and entranced his soul. From that first day of his discipleship it was John's chief delight to be in the company of his Master. Only for one brief moment, when sudden panic seized him at the flash of the lanterns in the garden, only for one brief moment did John leave Jesus. But love soon cast out fear and he followed his Lord to the Judgment Hall and never left his side till the bitter tragedy was over.

Yes, John was in the Judgment Hall a witness of the buffeting and the spitting. And John was with the Roman soldiers a witness of the scourging and the crowning. And John was at the foot of the Cross with the women—a witness of His dying. Yes, the last person upon whom the Lord's eye fell was the beloved disciple, and His last command was a command addressed to him. "Woman," Jesus said to Mary, "behold thy son." "Son," Jesus said to John, "behold thy mother."

Yes, whatever faults may be laid to John's account, and he had many, this much must be said to his credit—he loved Jesus with *all the passion and intensity of his soul*. And Jesus, I repeat, loved him for that. And Jesus still loves men for that. They may be full of faults laden with iniquity, but if love to Jesus is the deepest thing in their souls, they too are amongst the disciples whom Jesus loved.

The Work of Love

But see now what this love did for John. For love, as I have said more than once, is not a mere sentiment, it is not empty emotion. Love is power, love is a force, love is a mighty energy. Put the love of Christ into a man's soul, and you need not despair of reformation. Human love can do much to revolutionize character. Many a book has for its theme the difference which love made. George Eliot, in her *Silas Marner*, pictures an old man delivered from a blight of avarice and a hardened heart by the love of a little child. Many a young man has been delivered from the horrible pit and miry clay of impurity and lust by the love of a good woman. Yes, there is power in love. "For, indeed," says Tennyson, "I know

> *Of no more subtle Master under Heaven*
> *Than is the maiden passion for a maid,*
> *Not only to keep down the base in man*
> *But teach high thought and amiable words*
> *And courtliness and the desire of fame,*
> *And love of truth and all that makes a man."*

But I know of a more "Subtle Master" than even the "maiden passion for a maid," and that is the soul's passion for Jesus. Let that love enter into a man's heart, and it will work a more wondrous transformation than that of a boor into a gentle knight—it will change a sinner into a saint.

That potent and mighty love entered into John's heart, and little by little it transformed and transfigured him. "If any man is in Christ," writes the Apostle Paul, "he is a new creature; old things have passed away, all things have become new." And when John was in Christ he became *a new creature*. The contrast between the John of the Gospels and the John of the Epistles and the John of tradition is so tremendous, that we can scarcely believe they are all the same person.

Indeed, they are not the same. It is the old John, the aboriginal and natural John you meet with in the Gospels, it is the new man in Christ you meet with in the Epistles. The John of the Gospels is an ambitious man, seeking ever the chief place for himself; but the new man in Christ is a man of such modest and humble mind that never once does he mention his own name in the great Gospel that came from his pen. The John of the Gospels was a man eager to destroy; the new man in Christ is like his Lord, eager to serve.

One of the tenderest and most pathetic stories told of John is that which tells how he entrusted to a certain bishop the charge of a youth of promising qualities of mind. The youth, however, fell into evil company; and ended by becoming the leader of a band of assassins and robbers who struck terror into the whole country. When John returned to Ephesus he went to the bishop and demanded the precious deposit he had left in his hands. The bishop, with tears, told him what had befallen the youth. John instantly called for a horse and rode into the forest in which the robbers lay, and called to their

captain in tones of the most tender entreaty. He never stopped calling and praying till the young man had been melted into penitence,
had abandoned his evil behaving and had been reconciled again to
God.

The John of the Gospels is a selfish man, eager only for his own
advancement and aggrandizement, but the new man in Christ is a
man overflowing with kindness and love. Yes, by the end the Son of
Thunder has been changed into the Apostle of Love. "Love" is the
word that is ever upon John's lips now. God is love, he says, and he
that loveth is born of God and knoweth God. "A new commandment," he writes, "give I unto you—that ye love one another." That
was the last sermon he ever preached. He was carried into Church at
the last, and being too feeble to preach used to content himself with
saying, "Little children, love one another." And when his disciples,
weary of the continual repetition, asked why he always said that, he
replied, "Because it is our Lord's commandment, and if we fulfil this
alone, we have fulfilled all things."

Yes, beyond question love made a new man of John. Boanerges
became the Apostle of Love by loving Christ and living with Him.
And that love has lost none of its ancient power. Love Christ and
live with Him, and you will triumph over sin, and be changed into
newness of life. To attempt to reform yourselves, to lop off this evil
habit, to slay that foul appetite is terrible work. But admit the love of
Christ into your hearts, and working from the center, it will revolutionize the life.

"What are you?" said a gardener to a piece of fragrant clay in his
garden. "What are you? Are you a rose?"

"No," answered the clay, "but they laid me near a rose." Love
Christ and live with Him, and you shall catch His spirit; you shall be
changed into the same image from glory to glory.

Love and Insight

In conclusion, let me point out further how the Apostle of Love is
the Apostle of Vision and Insight. They say Love is blind. Never was
a bigger blunder made. Love is insight, love is knowledge, love is
vision, love lends quickness to the eyes. When Jesus walked along the
sea of Tiberias in the early dawn, it was love that recognized Him. "It
is the Lord," said John to Peter. And the same love that recognized

Jesus on the shore of the lake has seen deepest and furthest into the character of Jesus. For the fullest understanding of Jesus you must turn to the fourth Gospel. It was the man who loved Him most who knew Him best.

And this man who loved Jesus with all his soul was delivered forever from all fear of death. Death had no terrors for him. He could welcome it with exceeding great joy, for it did but restore him to the Lord for whom his heart panted and yearned. "Behold," said the messenger to him in the Isle of Patmos, "I come quickly." And John said in reply, with a shining face, "Even so, come quickly, Lord Jesus."

Dr. Andrew Bonar it was, I believe, who used to say that the ability to welcome the coming Christ was a fair test of love to Christ. It is a searching test. But John's love stood it. "Even so," said John, "come quickly, Lord Jesus."

Will our love stand this searching test? If the message reached us, "I come quickly," could we reply, "Even so come, Lord Jesus"? Beloved, inasmuch as we know neither the day nor the hour when the Son of Man will come, let us ask God to give us John's undivided and whole-souled love in order that we too, like him, may be amongst those who love our Lord's appearing.

5

ANDREW

"Andrew, Simon Peter's brother, was one of the two who heard what John had said and who had followed Jesus."

—*John 1:40 NIV*

I HAVE DISCOVERED Andrew's counterpart in the Old Testament: Andrew's prototype and forerunner is in one of the heroes of the Old Dispensation. The writer of the books of Samuel and the writer of the books of Chronicles both devote five verses or so out of their most romantic and fascinating histories to placing on record some account of Benaiah the son of Jehoiada.

Benaiah was one of David's mighty men of valor, and both historians have thought it worth while to preserve for us some of the exploits which won for him his reputation for daring courage, notably these two: that he went down and slew a lion in a pit on a snowy day, and that he slew an Egyptian, a man of five cubits high, though he had but a staff in his hand, while the Egyptian carried a spear which was like a weaver's beam.

Those were, indeed, great exploits; but after having carefully considered what the Bible says about Benaiah, I have come to the conclusion that his greatest exploit was one which is not even mentioned by the historians among his valorous deeds. This was Benaiah's chief exploit, this was his great feat and high achievement: that in a place calculated to foster envy and jealousy, Benaiah preserved a sunny disposition and a generous heart; that in a trying and even exasperating position he never allowed himself to become sullen or bitter. For, according to Scripture, this was the invidious and galling position Benaiah occupied—"Behold, he was more honorable than the thirty, but he attained not unto the first three" (1 Chronicles 11:25). Benaiah's achievements quite clearly lifted him up above the second rank, and yet, for some reason or other, he was not admitted into the first three. If I know anything of human nature I know this, that never did man occupy a harder position than Benaiah did. He was so near the very front rank, and yet not quite of it. You and I, had we been in his place, would have hated those first three. Yes, those three men just above us would have plagued the very life out of us.

Had Joab, the bloody son of Zeruiah, been in Benaiah's place, I would not have given a year's wages for the lives of the first three. One after the other they would have fallen victims to his treacherous and envious sword. But Benaiah—this man of large and generous heart—accepted his subordinate position without a murmur. He did not whine or sulk because, in spite of his brave and chivalrous deeds, David had passed him over. He accepted his position cheerfully; and a braver, more devoted, more whole-hearted servant than Benaiah the son of Jehoiada David never had.

"Better is he that ruleth his spirit," says the wise man, "than he that taketh a city." It is a greater feat and a nobler triumph to keep a meek and a quiet spirit, to cast out envy and malice and jealousy, that foul and hellish brood that haunts the heart, than it is to carry one's self bravely amid the clash and smoke of battle. A man's most terrible foes are those of his own household.

"The hardest fight I was ever in," so it is written on an old gravestone, "was the fight against self in the battle of sin." Benaiah came off victor in that most terrible and desperate encounter—the fight against Self. Yes, it was a great feat to slay a lion in a pit on a snowy day; it was a great feat to slay that Egyptian with his ponderous spear. But it was an infinitely greater feat to bear with a quiet and uncomplaining spirit the placing of these three over his head. Yes, that in his so terrible position—above the thirty, but not equal to the first three—Benaiah kept himself free from envy was, in very truth, a great achievement, a very miracle of the grace of God.

Andrew's Place among the Twelve

The place that Benaiah occupied among David's mighty men, Andrew occupied among the twelve: "Behold, he was more honor-

able than the eight, but he attained not unto the first three." Andrew
occupied an uncertain and most difficult position.

If you will look at the lists of the Apostles given to us in the
Gospels, you will find Andrew's name always mentioned in the first
group, along with Peter and James and John. And yet, when you
come to examine the Gospel history, you discover that he was certainly not on an equality with the great three. He was not admitted
into the intimacy of Christ as were they; he was not made a witness
of the great experiences of Christ as were they.

Andrew was left behind when Jesus took Peter and James and
John to witness His first struggle with the power of death in Jairus'
house. Andrew was left behind when Jesus took Peter and James and
John to behold His transfiguration glory on the Holy Mount. Andrew
was left behind when Jesus took Peter and James and John to share
His sorrow in the garden. His name is always reckoned in the first
group, and he obviously ranks higher than the remaining Apostles,
and yet he is not quite the peer of Peter and James and John. He
exactly reproduces Benaiah's position: "Behold he was more honorable than the eight, but he attained not to the first three." I do not
know why Andrew was not permitted to share in the privileges of
Peter and James and John. It may have been, as Dr. Cox suggests,
"that he was of a spirit less open and quick, less bold and adventurous
than the other three." But this I know, that of all places in the
Apostolate, this that Andrew held was the most calculated to test the
qualities of a man's soul. Andrew was "betwixt and between." He was
above the second, and not quite in the first rank. Of all places to test
a man's character, *that* was the place. It would have been an intolera-
ble place for James and John. With their keen and absorbing desire to
be first they would have turned sick with envy had they occupied
Andrew's position. But it is to Andrew's everlasting credit and honor
that, in this most trying and terrible place, he preserved the sweetness
and serenity of his temper. He did not mope or murmur when Peter
and James and John were taken and he was left. No trace of jealousy
found a lodging in his large and generous heart. He was content to be
passed over; he was content to fill a subordinate place.

Yes, I believe Andrew would have been quite content, had it been
the Lord's will, to take the lowest room. And that is Andrew's crowning grace and glory. He was not as gifted as Peter or James or John.
But he had that rare ornament, the brightest gem in the whole

chaplet of Christian graces—he had the ornament of a meek and a humble spirit. And in that great day, when judgment will go by character and not by gifts, when first shall be last and last first, it may be that this man Andrew, this self-forgetful, self-effacing Andrew, who never attained to the first three on earth, will be found amongst the chiefest in the Kingdom of God. With Andrew as my text, I feel I could preach a sermon about the "Love That Envieth Not." The longer I live, the more I learn to dread and hate that ugly, universal and well-nigh ineradicable sin of *envy.* "Love *envieth* not," says Paul. Applying that test, how many of us can lay claim to the possession of Christian love? How many of us? Is there anyone ready to assert that he carries within his breast a heart that harbors no particle of envy? What have you to say to this, men and women, "Love envieth not"? Can you lay claim to *love*? I do not wish to indulge in harsh judgments, but if my heart is at all an index to yours, there are some of us who, if we had been in Andrew's place, would never have slept, but would have had all our moments embittered by envy of Peter and James and John. For that terrible, that hateful, that miserable "envy which turns pale, and sickens even if a friend prevail," is in the hearts of us all. Yes, in the hearts of us *all.*

You, businessman, have you never envied your competitor who is doing a little better than you are? You, professional man, have you never envied that other professional man who has a greater reputation than you have? You, preacher, have you never envied your brother preacher who has larger congregations, and is more often noticed in the press than you are? You, woman, have you never been envious of your sister woman who happens to be younger and fairer and more admired than yourself? What are we to say to these questions? It is the most terrible reflection upon human nature, and the most convincing proof of the corruption and depravity of the human heart, that we cannot hear another person praised without a choking sensation in the throat and a sick feeling at the heart. This devil of envy is the last of the hellish brood to be driven from the human heart. The devil of lust may be driven out; the devil of lying may be cast forth; the devil of avarice may be torn from his seat; but this devil of envy still lurks even in pious and regenerate souls. The work of sanctification will be about completed in us when this evil spirit is purged out of our hearts, when we are able honestly to rejoice in the success and prosperity and reputation of others, and learn with Andrew in honor to prefer one another.

The Humble Place

I would also lift up this man Andrew, who attained not unto the first three, as an example of a man who thought more of service than of reputation, more of *the work to be done* than of the place given to the worker. There are some who will only work if they are put into prominent positions; they will not join the army unless they can be made officers. James and John had a good deal of that spirit; they wanted to be *first* in the kingdom. They and Peter and the rest were always wrangling about which should be greatest. But Andrew never took part in those angry debates; he had no craving for prominence. Andrew anticipated Christina Rossetti and said to his Lord:

> "Give me the lowest place; not that I dare
> Ask for that lowest place; but Thou hast died
> That I might live and share Thy glory by Thy side,
> Give me the lowest place; or if for me
> That lowest place be too high, may one more low,
> Where I may sit and see my God, and love Thee so."

It never troubled Andrew that he was not among the first three. It never distressed him that men talked more of Peter and James and John than they did of him. All Andrew thought of was *the work*. His reputation he was quite willing to leave to his Lord. "Men heed thee," he would often say to his soul, "love thee, praise thee not. The Master praises; what are men?"

Andrew is the type and father of all those who labor quietly in humble places—missionaries in far-off countries, pastors in tiny churches, humble Christians who are strangers to office, who do their faithful deed, content to be anonymous. And he makes his appeal to us, with our love of recognition and acknowledgment, to labor in the Christian vineyard not with eye service as men-pleasers, but as the servants of Christ, doing the will of God from the heart.

Now, this man of generous heart and humble mind, this man Andrew, was one of the two first disciples Jesus ever had. Andrew was a disciple of the Baptist before he became a disciple of the Christ. He was witness of the solemn scene in Jordan when Jesus came to be baptized of John. On the morrow after that never-to-be-forgotten day, John was standing with two of his disciples when Jesus passed.

John pointed to Him, and said to his two disciples, "Behold, the Lamb of God." And the two disciples heard him speak, and they followed Jesus.

When Jesus turned and beheld them following, He said to them, "What seek ye?" And they said unto Him, "Master, where abidest Thou?" He said unto them, "Come, and ye shall see." They came, therefore, saw where He abode, and they abode with Him that day; it was about the tenth hour.

One of the two who heard John speak and followed Him was Andrew, Simon Peter's brother. I should like to have had some record of what took place in our Lord's humble lodging that night. When I think of our Savior's wonderful conversation with Nicodemus, and His equally wonderful conversation with the Samaritan woman at the well, I feel I would give worlds to have had a report of the conversation that took place between Jesus and these seeking souls that night. It would be a never-to-be-forgotten conversation, I know; and just as Paul used to look back to the great light on the way to Damascus as the supreme experience of his life, so Andrew and John used to date everything back to this their first conversation with Jesus.

I do not know what He said; but as they listened to Him, their hearts—like that of John Wesley in the Moravian meeting house— were strangely warmed, and before they left, that night *they* had found their Messiah, and Jesus had found His first two disciples. Yes, let us never forget that to Andrew belongs that honor. He was "in Christ," as Paul would say, before his greater brother, Peter. Others might afterwards surpass him in gifts, but none could rob him of the glory of being the first to believe in Jesus.

Andrew—the Missionary

Having found Jesus, what did Andrew do? This. *The first disciple became the first missionary.* Yes, that is what the very next verse reveals to us—Andrew, the newly made disciple, became a missionary of the Faith. When a man has found Christ and really tasted the joys of His salvation, he feels he must communicate his discovery. "Let the redeemed of the Lord *say so*," sings one Psalmist; and the redeemed, I will add, simply cannot help saying so. "I have not hid Thy righteousness within my heart, I have *declared* Thy righteousness and

Thy salvation," sings another Psalmist. Yes, when a man has experienced the salvation of God the word is like a fire in his bones, and *he must declare* it.

"We cannot but speak," answered Peter and John, when charged not to teach or preach in the name of Jesus. "We cannot but speak." A man cannot be dumb, he cannot keep silence, when once he has felt the redeeming love and power of Jesus Christ.

It was even thus with Andrew. He had been waiting for the Messiah for years, and at last he had found Him! Andrew was beside himself with joy that night, and his joy craved to impart itself. There were hundreds of others in Galilee who were watching and waiting for Christ. To them the news that He had come would be as welcome as bread to the hungry or water to those who were perishing of thirst. Andrew could scarce contain himself as he thought of them. When they left Christ's lodging and passed out into the night, Andrew said to John, "John, this is a day of good tidings; let us go and tell." And Andrew went and told! Yes, for sheer eagerness he ran that night to tell to other anxious and waiting souls this good news: "We have found Him of whom Moses and the prophets did write."

In this respect Andrew was a model disciple. I do not know that he could have preached an eloquent sermon such as his brother Peter was able to preach in later days. But it did not need eloquence to announce good news; the good news is eloquence enough in itself. Lepers appeared once in the famine-stricken streets of Samaria, and shouted to its fainting and perishing people, "Bread in plenty yonder!" And the Samaritans never heard oratory so sweet. A man galloped into the market place of a Dutch town on a horse white with foam, and gasped one word: "Free!" But these citizens never heard speech more eloquent than that. So Andrew went and said, "We have found Messiah" and weary hearts grew hopeful once again. And in this respect, I repeat, Andrew was a *model disciple*. For we are saved that we may save others; we are called that we may be *sent*; we are made disciples that we may become *apostles*.

You who are redeemed of the Lord—have you *said* so? You who have tasted the joys of God's salvation, have you *declared* it? You who are called to be disciples—have you become apostles yet? To how many have you carried the good news of what Jesus has done for *your* soul? To how many have you gone and said, like Andrew, "We have found the Messiah"? Every Christian disciple a Christian mission-

ary—that is what Christ looks for; and missionaries all of us can be.
To be a missionary one need not be a preacher, or even a teacher in
the Sunday school. To be a Christian missionary is within the com-
pass of even the humblest of us, for this is the missionary's business—to
testify to others: "We have found the Christ."

The Missionary to the Home

Notice another thing. When Andrew began his missionary activity, he began it *in his own home*. This is what the Gospel says: "He
findeth first his own brother Simon, and saith unto him, We have
found the Messiah. He brought him unto Jesus." In going to his own
home, Andrew, I will venture to say, went *to the most difficult place of
all*. I do not know whether I am expressing your feelings or not, but I
feel it is easier to go as a missionary to the heathen than it is to be a
missionary to one's own home! It is far easier to preach from the
pulpit to a crowd, or to speak to a class in the Sunday school, than it
is to speak a loving word to brother or sister, father or mother, son or
daughter in the home. Yet it is in the home Christ would have us
begin work for Him.

You remember what He said to the man out of whom He had cast
a legion of devils, and who, in his gratitude, wished to remain at
Jesus' side: "Go home," said Jesus, "go home to thy friends, and tell
them what great things the Lord hath done for thee." He was to
become a missionary, and his first sphere of service was to be *his own
home*. That is exactly what Andrew did without being ordered—he
became a missionary to his own home. "He findeth *first* his own
brother Simon. And he brought him to Jesus."

Missionaries, that is what Christ wants us all to be. And whither will
He send us? Where He sent the Gadarene of old—*to our own homes*.
And what a fine field of labor the home affords! Father and mother,
have you no son or daughter who has not yet found Christ? Will you
not tell them what great things the Lord has done for your souls?
Young men and women, have you no brothers or sisters or parents who
are still strangers to Christ? Will you not speak to them and tell them
all He has been to you, and how He had compassion upon you? The
home, the home— there is no finer field for missionary service.

How is it Christian parents have wicked and godless children?
How is it we see Christian young people with irreligious brothers and

sisters? Could it be that the home is a neglected mission field? Oh, let us all become imitators of Andrew. We parents should accustom ourselves to speak to our children, for some day we could be asked whether we talked with our children and wept over them, and prayed for them and with them, and did our very best for them. Upon us all—fathers and mothers, husbands and wives, sons and daughters, brothers and sisters—Christ lays the command: "Go home to thy friends, and tell them what great things the Lord hath done for thee."

Andrew went home and told Peter, and *he brought him to Jesus*. Peter was a greater man than Andrew; but I am tempted to say that just as there might have been no Paul but for Barnabas, so there would have been no Peter but for Andrew. God only knows what may result from the simple word of even a humble Christian. A lady's kindly invitation called John Williams to the great missionary cause in the South Seas. A Primitive Methodist minister's sermon gave Charles Spurgeon to the church to become the "prince of preachers." And so Andrew's simple missionary work at home gave Peter the Rock, the Prince and primate of the Twelve, to the Primitive Church. One never knows what far-reaching results may issue from a simple testimony.

> *"Speak for the love of God,*
> *Speak for the love of man;*
> *The words of truth love sends abroad*
> *Can never be in vain."*

Andrew's Wider Labors

But Andrew's labors were not confined to his own home. We read elsewhere in the Gospels that he was the means of introducing a group of *Greeks* to Jesus who were so anxious to see Him. Nothing stirred our Lord's soul as did the coming of those Greeks. They were the firstfruits of the Gentiles, and in vision Christ saw the kingdom stretching from shore to shore and from the river unto the ends of the earth.

It was Andrew who brought them. I have come to the conclusion that Andrew was not much of a preacher. Not a single sermon of his has been recorded for us. But he was an *embodied introduction*. He delighted to bring individuals into contact with Christ. He was great at *personal work*. And in this way he did, perhaps, more good than he could have done by the most brilliant preaching. At any rate, he did his very best, and there will be many a bright gem in Andrew's crown in the day when the Lord shall number up His jewels.

"He attained not unto the first three." No, not in genius and gift. Andrew never became a great leader or a famous preacher. But with his humbler gifts he did his best; and in the whole circle of the Apostolate, Jesus did not have a more faithful and devoted servant. Andrew sits upon his throne today. And Andrew is an appeal to the "two-talent" people who are not geniuses—just to be faithful and do their best.

John Williams, who was martyred, speaking in Edinburgh once thrilled a missionary meeting with an account of his wonderful work in the islands of the sea. After him a meek, trembling fellow-missionary had to speak, and this was how he began: "My friends, I have no remarkable success to relate like Mr. Williams. I have labored for Christ in a far-off sphere for years, and have seen but small result of my toil; but this is my comfort: When the Master comes to reckon with his servants, He will not say, 'Well done, thou good and successful servant,' but 'Well done, thou good and *faithful* servant.' I have tried to be faithful."

This is the key. It is on fidelity that the blessing is pronounced; and therefore the blessing may be ours. Andrew attained not unto the first three, but because he did his best he sits on his throne beside Peter and James and John today. Famous and brilliant we may not be. But we can all be faithful.

That is the question I would put to you, with Andrew as my text: "Are you doing your very best for Jesus Christ? Are you honestly doing all you can to extend His kingdom and advance His cause?"

We have sung scores of times, "Take myself, and I will be, Ever only, all for Thee." Ever only—all for Christ! Have we been that? Have we done our best? If we have we are blessed, for to us our Lord will one day say, "Well done, good and faithful servant; thou hast been faithful in a few things, I will make thee ruler over many things: enter thou into the joy of the Lord."

6

PHILIP

"The next day Jesus decided to leave for Galilee. Finding Philip, he said to him, 'Follow me.' Philip, like Andrew and Peter, was from the town of Bethsaida." —John 1:43, 44 NIV

"NOW PHILIP WAS from Bethsaida . . . the city of Andrew and Peter." In that simple matter-of-fact statement the Evangelist sums up all that he thinks it necessary for us to know concerning Philip prior to the time of his calling and Apostleship.

It is, of course, interesting to know the town to which Philip belonged, but the information does not at first glance seem to help us much in our understanding of the man. Nevertheless, I am convinced that it is not for nothing that the Evangelist has put it on record that Philip belonged to Bethsaida, the city of Andrew and Peter. The Evangelists are economists of space, and are not in the habit of recording *unimportant* facts, however interesting; they only record what is vital.

This fact that Philip came from Bethsaida, the city of Andrew and Peter, has been preserved because it has some close connection with and some vital bearing upon Philip's spiritual history. It is not safe to assume that you have taken in the whole meaning of even the simplest Scripture statement at first glance. "There's a deep below the deep and a height above the height." Even its plainest and apparently most obvious sentences have their buried treasures to be discovered if only we will study them closely enough and ponder over them long enough.

"In the year that King Uzziah died I saw the Lord," writes Isaiah in that magnificent and most moving chapter in which he relates the story of his call. "In the year that King Uzziah died," says the prophet, and as we read that sentence we are tempted at first sight to think that he is here merely fixing a date—just as we date our letters, "in the year of our Lord, 1901." "No," says Professor George Adam Smith, "this is much more than a *date*. This is an *experience*." The death of Uzziah was the supreme and decisive experience of the prophet's life. Had not Uzziah died it is possible that he might never have seen the Lord at all.

"Now Philip was from Bethsaida . . . the city of Andrew and Peter," says John; and as we read that sentence we are inclined at first glance just to regard it as a geographical note—Philip's postal address, so to speak. No! this is more than a geographical note; this is a link in Philip's spiritual history. This is more than the mention of the place of Philip's abode; this gives us the clue and key to Philip's religious development.

The important part of the sentence is not that Philip was from Bethsaida, but that Bethsaida was the city of Andrew and Peter. This sentence links Philip with Andrew and Peter. It reveals to us not his mere dwelling, but—what is infinitely more important—his *friend-ships*. These friendships shaped and molded his character, and so led to his new birth and his Apostolic calling. It was Philip's good fortune, it was his happy lot, to live in the same town and to count among his friends those two eminent saints of God, Andrew and Peter, the sons of Jonas.

The Influence of the Saints

It is well, it is indeed an unspeakable blessing, to live under the same roof, or in the same street, or even in the same town with some people. They are so supremely, so radiantly good that their mere presence in a town is a benediction. Virtue streams out of them to bless and purify and gladden all with whom they come in contact.

It must have been a blessed thing to live in Assisi in those far-off days when Francis came preaching his gospel of a simple faith, and appealing to men to seek first the Kingdom of God and His righteousness. It must have been a most blessed thing to live in Florence in those high and heroic days when Savonarola had inspired the

Florentines to make Jesus Christ their King. It must also have been a great privilege to have lived in Geneva in those great days when John Calvin sought to realize and actualize in that Swiss town the holy city of God. It must have been a rare privilege to have been a student at Edinburgh University in those days when Henry Drummond held his memorable meetings there. For to know these men, to come within the sweep of their influence, to touch but the hem of their garments, was to be blessed and purified and strengthened.

Yes, I will believe that in heaven today there are many who, when asked the question, "What brought them to that world above, that heaven so bright and fair?" will give this for answer: "We were of Assisi, the city of Francis. We were of Florence, the city of Savonarola. We were of Geneva, the city of John Calvin. We were of Edinburgh, the city of Henry Drummond." It is to their contact with these men that—under God—they ascribe their eternal salvation.

And so I verily believe, that could we ask Philip how he came to sit on one of the twelve heavenly thrones, and to have his name engraved on one of the twelve foundations of the Eternal City, he would return this answer: "I was from Bethsaida, of the city of Andrew and Peter." Under God, Philip owed his soul to Andrew and Peter, and especially to Andrew.

In Scripture you will find Philip closely associated with Andrew. It was to Andrew, Philip always went in his difficulties, for Andrew was none other than his father in the faith. Andrew will have many a bright gem to his crown in the day that Jesus numbers up His jewels, and among them will be his fellow-Apostle, Philip. Yes, it was well for Philip; it was to Philip's eternal salvation that he lived in Bethsaida in the days of Andrew and Peter. Andrew and Peter were poor and humble fishermen, but they were also more than fishermen. They were earnest and serious men. They looked for the hope of Israel. Expectantly they watched for the coming of Messiah.

From these two men there spread to others in Bethsaida a contagion of holy expectancy, and among others to catch the contagion was Philip. Yes, Philip was delivered from the fascinations of the world and led to watch and wait for Messiah by the example and influence of Simon Peter. "*Si, Stephanus non orasset,*" said Augustine in a noted sentence, "*ecclesia Paulum non haberet*"—"the Church would never have had Paul but for the prayer of Stephen." And looking at this sentence, that Philip was from Bethsaida, of the city of

Andrew and Peter, and considering what is implied by it and in-
volved in it, I will make bold to say, "The Church would never have
had Philip but for Andrew and Peter." Philip might have imitated
the example of that Englishman, and asked—as he did—that these
words be engraved upon his tombstone: "I had a friend." Yes, Philip
had a friend, and he owed everything to that fact. Here is the key to
Philip's spiritual history: "Now Philip was from Bethsaida, of the city
of Andrew and Peter."

When I consider what a blessing the presence of Andrew and
Peter in Bethsaida proved to be to their fellow-townsman Philip, I am
compelled to put this question to you as I would put it to myself: "Are
we a means of blessing to the people who live under the same roof
with us, in the same street with us, in the same town with us?"

Our Lord clearly contemplated our becoming centers of healing,
cleansing, gladdening influence. He uses two figures to describe our
duty and function in the world. He speaks of His people in one place
as "the salt" of the earth, the preservative against rottenness and
corruption. Have you acted as "the salt"? Have you ever come between anyone and moral corruption? Have you ever saved anyone
from decay and rottenness and putrefaction? He speaks of His people
in another place as "the light of the world"—gladsome, purifying,
revealing light. Have you ever acted as the "light" to anyone? Have
you ever given guidance in darkness? Have you been a center of
gladdening and purifying influence?

Has your mere presence been a blessing to your home, your friends,
your town? Will there be any in the eternal mansions ready to at-
tribute their attainment to those "seats of everlasting bliss" to our
influence upon them? Will there be anyone to say, "I came from the
same town as So-and-so"; "I lived in the same shop with So-and-so";
"I numbered So-and-so in the circle of my friends"? Will there be
anyone to say that of us? To have even one able to say that of us is
not to have lived in vain. For know this, that "he that hath convert-
ed a sinner from the error of his ways, hath saved a soul from death
and shall cover a multitude of sins."

The Finding of Philip

"On the morrow"—the morrow, that is, after the call of Andrew—
Jesus was minded to go forth into Galilee, and He found Philip, and

Jesus saith unto him, "Follow Me." *"He findeth Philip."* Scripture is rather fond of that word "find," but let us be careful what ideas we read into it.

"Jesus *findeth* Philip." How? By accident? No. By coincidence? No. There is no room in the world for chance or accident. It was inevitable that Jesus and Philip should meet—inevitable, I say, unless the promises of God are a delusion and a snare. To realize the inevitableness, the absolute necessity of this meeting—you should read John 1:44 before verse 43. "Now Philip was from Bethsaida, of the city of Andrew and Peter." What does that mean? It means that Philip belonged to that little company of faithful souls who watched and waited for the coming of the Lord; it meant that, like Simeon, he was looking for the consolation of Israel.

In a word, Philip was a *seeker*. The connection between *seeking* and *finding* is regarded in Holy Scripture as possessing all the inevitability of natural law. The one is regarded as the invariable and necessary sequence of the other. "If thou seek Him," said David in his charge to Solomon, "if thou seek Him, He will be found of you." "Ye shall seek Me and find Me," said Jeremiah of the Lord, "when ye shall search for Me with all your heart." "Seek," said Jesus Christ, "and ye shall find." As certainly and inevitably as day follows night and spring follows summer—by a law as invariable and immutable as the law of gravitation—*he who seeks, finds.*

There was no accident, therefore, in this meeting of Jesus and Philip. Unless God's word can be broken and flouted and set aside, it was inevitable that they should. For Philip was a seeking soul, and every seeking soul finds in the long run. Philip found. After his first interview with Jesus he ran to his friend Nathaniel to tell him that the long and weary search was at last at an end. "Eureka!" he cried, as he burst in upon Nathaniel's meditation. "We *have found* Him of whom Moses in the Law and the prophets did write." And with Philip as my text, I will preach with all boldness and confidence this blessed truth: Every soul who seeks shall find.

There are some searches in which men have engaged which have had failure at the end of them. They have sought for the elixir of life, and failed. They have searched for that wondrous stone which was to change everything it touched into gold, and failed. They have sent expedition after expedition to search for the North Pole, and failed. But here is a search that *never* fails. "They that seek Me shall *find*

Me." Yes, I give it on the sure word of our Lord Jesus Christ: "Every one who seeks finds." Today there are seeking souls everywhere. This is a seeking age. "O God, show Thyself!" is its cry. There are those whose hearts cry out: "Oh, that I knew where I might find Him, that I might come even to His seat!" Listen to me, for I have a Gospel—good news for you. Your searching will end in finding. Yes, if you are in real earnest about it, the day will come when you will acquaint yourselves with God and be at peace. The happy day will dawn when you too, like Philip, will be able to cry, "We have found Him for whom our hearts panted and languished and yearned."

"*Every one* that seeketh findeth"; therefore, seek on, and be not discouraged, though the time of search be long and dreary, and say this word every day for the comfort and encouragement of your souls, "Every one who seeks finds."

There was a time in John Bunyan's experience when the Tempter tried to persuade him that neither the mercy of God nor the blood of Christ did at all concern him, and therefore it was but in vain to pray. "Yet," said Bunyan to himself, "I will pray."

"But," said the Tempter, "your sin is unpardonable."

"Well," said Bunyan, "I will pray."

"It will not help," the Tempter said.

"Yet," replied that much-tried saint, "I will pray."

In much the same way the Tempter will seek to persuade you that your search is in vain. "Yet," do you say unto him, "I will seek." "But," he will say, "God is past finding out." "Still," do you answer him, "I will seek." "But," he will urge, "it will not help." "Nevertheless," do you make reply, "I will seek." Be resolved to seek on. Live seeking and die seeking, and I will pledge God Almighty's word that soon or late you will be satisfied with His likeness, and you will know Him whom to know is life eternal.

Philip the Inquirer

What kind of man was this Philip who so happily found Christ and was found by Him? Well, Scripture does not tell us very much about him—indeed it only mentions him three times outside this chapter in John; but those three references, together with what we read here, give a consistent portrait and reveal Philip to us, above everything else, as a man of an *inquiring mind*. The patient inquirer comes out in the description of Jesus he gives to Nathaniel. "We have found Him," says Philip, "of whom Moses in the Law and the Prophets did write." Andrew and John followed Christ on the testimony of the Baptist and at the bidding of their own hearts. But Philip accepted Him, and followed because he found that Christ satisfies the descriptions given in the Old Testament.

Yes, Philip brought out Moses and the prophets and tested Christ by them and accepted Him, because he saw that what they had written was fulfilled in Him.

The same habit of patient and accurate examination and inquiry comes out in the incident of the feeding of the five thousand. At a certain point in the day's proceedings, Jesus turned to Philip with the question, "Where are we to buy bread that these may eat?" This He said to prove him. Jesus knew His disciple; He knew his inquiring mind. He knew that Philip would have been making his computations. And so he had. "Two hundred pennyworth of bread," answered Philip promptly, "is not sufficient for them that every one of them may eat a little." Philip had been working it all out in his head, and he was ready with his answer.

It was for his inquiring and candid mind, probably, that the Greeks chose him out of all the Apostles as the one to whom they would make their request to see Jesus. "Their turning to him," says Lange, "depended upon a law of kindly attraction." Philip's own inquiring spirit would naturally put him in sympathy with these inquiring Greeks. And the same inquiring temper comes out in that memorable request Philip made in the Upper Room on the night in which Jesus was betrayed, "Lord, show us the Father, and it sufficeth us."

That, then, is the Philip of the Gospels—a man of inquiring and interrogative mind, a man intent upon proving and testing everything. And in that respect I have thought Philip is typical of this age in which we live. This, too, is an inquisitive and inquiring age. It is the age of the investigator and the critic. "The coat of arms of this age," says Dr. Van Dyke, "is an interrogation point, and its motto is *Query*."

Including this man Philip in the ranks of the twelve is a plain intimation to us that there is a place in the Church of Christ for the student and the critic, and that there is a work for them to do. This has not always been recognized, and the one who has taken upon himself to ask questions, and to investigate traditions, and to examine foundations, has often been treated as if he were a heathen and a publican. The critic is in our midst today; he is asking his questions—questions that affect some of our most cherished beliefs, and the Church is in no small distress because of him. We hear hard words used about him, and in some religious assemblies an attack upon the critics is an infallible method of calling forth applause.

I do not agree with all that the critics this day are saying; but I wish to indicate their place in the Church, and I desire to claim them as true servants of the Church. Philip had a place among the twelve, and the thoughtful critics of today are his lineal successors. They have rights in the Church, and they have rendered and are rendering true service to the Church. This twofold service the Philips of the Church have rendered: (1) They have brought us to the light and knowledge which we enjoy today. Yes, we owe our present rich inheritance of knowledge to the men who have ever cried, "Light, more light!" and who have believed that God has constantly "more light and truth to break forth from His word." And (2) they compel us to think for ourselves, so that our faith is no longer a matter of hearsay and tradition, but of conviction and experience. But for these men of inquiring mind we should sink into mental sloth. They provoke us to read and study and think, however, so that in due time we become able to give a reason for the faith that is in us, and so to stand foursquare against the winds that blow.

Philip the Man of Limited Vision

Philip was a man of inquiring mind, a man who made much of proofs and tests; but he had also the defects of his qualities; for he was a man of limited vision. "Seeing was believing" with Philip. Take the incident of the feeding of the five thousand. When Jesus asked him what they should do for bread, Philip never for one moment thought of his Master, but answered, in the most prosaic and matter-of-fact way, that at the very least it would take two hundred pennyworth of bread even to give a scanty meal to that vast crowd.

Philip never gave a thought to the Divine power; the feeding of the multitude was to him just a matter of pounds, shillings, and pence. The same trait in his character comes out in that memorable request he made of Jesus on the night of the betrayal: "Lord, show us the Father, and it sufficeth us." Philip wanted an actual theophany.

He had walked with Christ for three years and had never the eye to see the hidden glory beneath the seamless robe.

"Have I been so long with you, and hast thou not known *Me*, Philip? He that hath seen Me, hath seen the Father." That is precisely the peril in which critics and investigators stand today. Lacking imagination and vision, they are ruled and dominated by dates and facts and theories. "Seeing is believing" with them. They leave no room for the miraculous and the Divine. And yet when I read the conclusions of some critics—greatly though I deplore them—I can yet possess my soul in patience. For, just as Philip, this man of limited vision, came at last to the full knowledge of the truth, so I believe that our modern Philips, loving truth as they do, will come to the light, and will fall down at Jesus' feet crying, "My Lord, and my God!"

One more word I will add. It was a sign and proof of limited vision; but, for one, I am everlastingly grateful to Philip for asking that question, "Show us the Father, and it sufficeth us." Had it not been for that question, we should never have heard that gracious and beautiful word: "He that hath seen Me, hath the Father." But for Philip, we should never have heard it stated so plainly and unequivocally from the lips of our Lord Himself—that His pity and tenderness and love and self-sacrifice are the pity and tenderness and love and self-sacrifice of God.

Have you seen the Father—the tender, pitying, merciful Father? Yes, you have seen the mighty God, for His eternal power and Godhead are revealed by the things that are made. You can see His wisdom, His might, His strength in earth and sea and sky. But have you ever seen God's heart? Have you ever realized that He looks upon you as His dear children? Have you ever realized that He loves you as you love your little ones?

To know God like that is to have a quiet heart. Yes, once we are shown the Father, it is sufficient for us. Have we seen the Father? Would we like to see Him? Well, come and gaze on Jesus Christ— come and contemplate His love and His compassion and His measureless self-sacrifice. He who has seen Christ, has seen the Father. "Follow Me," said Jesus to Philip, and Philip arose and He was a man of very imperfect faith and limited knowledge; but he recognized one in Jesus who deserved to be followed, and he followed Him on the spot.

"Follow Me," says Christ to you and me. We may not have mastered all the subtleties of theology; like Philip, we may not even realize to the full the glory of Christ, but at any rate we see in Him the one Leader and Guide of souls. Let us follow Him, therefore. Let us say with the poet—

> *"If Jesus Christ is a man,*
> *And only a man, I say,*
> *That of all mankind I cleave to Him,*
> *And to Him will I cleave alway.*
>
> *If Jesus Christ is a God,*
> *And the only God, I swear*
> *I will follow Him though heaven and hell,*
> *The earth, the sea, and the air!"*

And following Him, like Philip, we will come into the light. "He that followeth Me shall not walk in darkness, but shall have the light of life."

7

BARTHOLOMEW

"When Jesus saw Nathanael approaching he said of him, 'Here is a true Israelite, in whom there is nothing false.'"—John 1:47 NIV

I ACCEPT THE judgment of the best and most trustworthy commentators, and identify the man Nathanael, to whom Christ pays this striking and splendid tribute, with that Bartholomew whose name is mentioned in the various lists of the Apostles next to the name of Philip.

It was no unusual thing for an Apostle to possess two names. Simon was also called Peter; Levi was known to the church as Matthew; another of the twelve rejoiced in the threefold appellation of Lebbaeus, Thaddaeus and Jude! There is, therefore, no *à priori* impossibility or even improbability about the suggestion that the sixth Apostle may have also possessed two names, especially when we remember that Bartholomew (Bar-Tohnai), like Bar-Jona, is only a patronymic or surname.

While, on the one hand, the occurrence of two names creates no difficulty, there are several positive considerations which point strongly to the identification of the Nathanael of the fourth Gospel with the Bartholomew of the other three. Let me state briefly what those considerations are:

Nathanael is mentioned twice in John's Gospel—in this first chapter, namely, and in the last. In this first chapter we have the account of his call. All the others whose calls are related in this opening chapter—Andrew, John, Peter, Philip—became in due time Apostles of Jesus Christ, and the inclusion of the account of Nathanael's call

75

in the same chapter with theirs naturally and inevitably suggests that he too in later days, like them, was numbered among the twelve Apostles. If Nathanael was not an Apostle, it is difficult to understand why, in his very opening chapter, John should have devoted seven verses to an account of his call.

But if the first chapter of the fourth Gospel makes it *probable* that Nathanael was an Apostle, the last chapter of the same Gospel puts the fact almost beyond doubt. In that chapter Nathanael is introduced as one of the "disciples," and, judging from the context, by "disciples" the Evangelist apparently means "Apostles." He is introduced as the friend and companion of the Apostles Peter and James and John and Thomas; and further, he is introduced as fulfilling a distinctively Apostolic function—that is, witnessing one of the post-resurrection appearances of Jesus Christ. Altogether, a study of the references to Nathanael in the fourth Gospel compels us to believe that in him we have one of the Apostles under another name.

But if Nathanael was an Apostle, which of the Apostles was he? Well, he could not have been Peter or Andrew or Philip, because they are mentioned along with him in this chapter. And he could not have been James or John or Thomas, because they are mentioned along with him in chapter 21. And he could not have been Matthew, for we know Matthew's other name was Levi; nor James the Less, for James was a relative of Christ's, while Nathanael is introduced here as a stranger to Him. And he certainly was not the traitor; and he could not be the other Judas, because he is mentioned in the fourth Gospel.

Thus, by a process of natural selection, the choice becomes limited to two. If Nathanael was an Apostle at all, he must have been either Bartholomew or Simon the Canaanite. Now there is absolutely nothing in the Gospels to lead us to identify him with Simon; but there *is* one fact at least to point to his identification with Bartholomew, and that is his association with Philip.

If you will turn to the lists of the Apostles in the Gospels you will find that in the lists of Matthew, Mark and Luke the names of Philip and Bartholomew come together. This is how the lists run: Simon and Andrew, James and John, Philip and Bartholomew. Philip and Bartholomew were companion Apostles. Now, if you will look at what John says here, you will notice that the first thing Philip did when he had found Christ himself was to run and tell Nathanael, and from that fact we are justified in concluding that Nathanael was Philip's bosom friend. Putting the two facts together it seems perfectly natural to find in Philip's companion Apostle, Bartholomew, this man Nathanael whom he was the means of bringing to Christ.

I shall, therefore, in all that I have to say in this chapter, regard Bartholomew and Nathanael as being one and the same person. All that we are told about Nathanael, Philip's friend, is told us in these seven verses of the first chapter of John's Gospel. Beyond these verses we do not read of a single act that Bartholomew ever did or a single word he ever said. But though these seven verses are all, they are quite sufficient—so suggestive and illuminating are they—to tell us what manner of man Nathanael was.

Nathanael the Man of Prayer

The first thing I will say about Nathanael is this—that he was a man much given to *study* and *meditation* and *prayer*. From the fact that his name occurs in the list of those who decided to return with Peter to his fishing, I gather that Nathanael, like most of his brother Apostles, was by trade or occupation a *fisherman*. But Nathanael never allowed himself to become absorbed in his business. He fished for a livelihood, but his heart was set on things above. Every moment that he could snatch from the demands of his daily toil he devoted to *quiet meditation* and *prayer*.

There was a circle of praying souls in Israel at this time, composed of men like Simeon, who looked for the consolation of Israel, and women like Anna, who departed not from the Temple, worshiping (with fastings and supplications) night and day. Of that elect and holy circle this man Nathanael was one. He had a garden attached to his humble home, and in that garden there was a fig tree; and underneath the leafy shade of that fig tree he would spend hour after hour—now upon his knees crying to God, now studying with utter absorption of soul what Moses in the Law and the Prophets did write.

So entirely was Nathanael given up to meditation and prayer, that if he was not in his boat upon the lake his friends knew they would be sure to find him under the fig tree in his garden. Yes, be sure his friends knew all about that fig tree. And not his friends only, but the angels in heaven also knew all about that fig tree. To their holy eyes the earth contained no more beautiful spot than the corner of

Nathanael's garden where that fig tree grew. And it was not his friends and the angels in heaven only, but our Lord too who knew all about that fig tree before ever He set eyes upon Nathanael's face. "Before Philip called thee, when thou wast under the fig tree, I saw thee." That fig tree was Nathanael's oratory, his upper room, his secret cell.

The Place of Prayer

"Pray always in the same place," says William Law in his *Serious Call.* "Pray always in the same place; reserve that place for devotion, and never allow yourself to do anything common in it." Isaac had his special place—it was the green field. Elijah had his special place—it was the mountain cave. Jesus had His special place—it was Gethsemane's garden. And Nathanael, too, had his special place—it was the fig tree. He reserved that place for devotion. Underneath that fig tree Nathanael was always either absorbed in meditation or upon his knees in prayer.

"Pray always in the same place; reserve that place for devotion." "This," adds Law, "would dispose you to be always in the right spirit when you were there, and fill you with wise and holy thoughts when you were by yourself." Have you, beloved, any special place set apart for devotion? Have you anything in your home corresponding to Nathanael's fig tree? "Yes, I know a person may pray anywhere, and all places are really equally sacred. But often enough the one who says he can pray *anywhere* ends by praying *nowhere*, and the one who asserts that all places are sacred, ends by making every place common. On the same principle and for the same reason that we mark Sunday as specially sacred—do you reserve some place for devotion? "Enter into thy closet," says Christ, "and pray." Yes, be sure you have some closet, some inner chamber, some fig tree, some little nook, that you keep as a place of meditation and prayer.

Nathanael not only had a place set aside for prayer, but he was himself full of the *spirit of prayer*. He was of the kindred of that Psalmist who wrote: "Oh, how love I Thy law: in Thy law do I meditate day and night."

"Pray without ceasing," said the great Apostle Paul, writing to the Thessalonians. And if he had been asked to quote an example of what he meant, I am persuaded he would have pointed to his brother

Apostle, Bartholomew (Nathanael), with his deep and unwearying delight in meditation and prayer.

William Law, in his great and noble book to which I have already referred, urges Christian people to abridge their time for sleep in order to have time for prayer. We need to pray in the fresh and early morning, and again at nine o'clock, and again at twelve o'clock, and again at three o'clock, and again at six o'clock, and again before retiring for the night.

Centuries before William Law came on the scene, Nathanael had done all and more than all that he recommends in his noble book. Yes, sometimes, like our Lord, Nathanael would be up and under his fig tree a long time before day; and at other times, like Paul and Silas in the dungeon at Philippi, Nathanael sang praises unto God under his fig tree at midnight. Yet again, like his Master, Nathanael many a time and often spent whole nights under the fig tree making supplication to God with strong crying and tears.

All this was not under the constraint of any such rules as William Law lays down, but just because his heart and flesh cried out for the living God, just because in God's presence and fellowship he found fulness of joy.

The Spirit of Prayer

Much as I desire that, like Nathanael, you should have your *place* of prayer, I desire much more that, like Nathanael, you should have this *spirit* of prayer, this keen and eager delight in the fellowship of God. To have the place without the spirit is of no avail.

"Prayer," says the old hymn—and we have often sung the verse "Prayer is the soul's sincere desire"—the soul's *sincere desire!* Is that so? Is it *your* soul's sincere desire? Is it what you long and yearn for most? Is it what your heart and flesh cry out for? Did you ever rise a long time before day in order to pray? Did you ever find midnight overtake you absorbed in love and praise? Have you ever wrestled with God the whole night through in agonizing prevailing prayer?

The soul's *sincere desire!* Is prayer so delightful to you that you snatch every moment you can spare in order that you may enjoy this blessed privilege? Unfortunately for many of us prayer is nothing but a task and a duty. Because we do not delight in it, we put no heart into it. We spend very few moments upon it. There must be nothing we want more than a baptism into Nathanael's spirit, so that we may find in fellowship and prayer our chief delight, and in God our highest joy, and be able with Isaac Watts to say—

> *"Thou art the sea of love*
> *Where all my pleasures roll,*
> *The circle where my passions move,*
> *And center of my soul."*

Nathanael the Man of Preconceived Opinions

The second point I want you to notice about Nathanael is that he was a man who had *imbibed the current and popular notions of Messiah*. Nathanael was a great student of Scripture, but he had studied it, shall I say, through the spectacles of the rabbis. He was looking for the Messiah, but the Messiah he looked for was not the Suffering Servant of Isaiah 53, not a man of sorrows and acquainted with grief; the Messiah Nathanael looked for was the Messiah he had been taught by the rabbis to expect—a great prince, clothed in purple, surrounded by all the pomp and splendor of royalty.

Thus it happened that when his friend Philip burst in upon him one day under the fig tree with the announcement, "We have found Him of whom Moses in the Law and the Prophets did write, Jesus of Nazareth, the son of Joseph," that Nathanael's preconceived notions would not allow him to believe the message, and he asked incredulously, "Can any good thing come out of Nazareth?"

Nathanael's own preconceived ideas—his prejudices, if you like—were the greatest obstacle in the way of his acceptance of the Gospel message. John Bunyan, with that incomparable insight of his, has noted the terrible part Prejudice plays in the lives of men. In his allegory, *The Holy War*—which, if he had not also written *Pilgrim's Progress,* would be counted the greatest allegory in the world—he pictures the soul as a walled city having five gates—Ear-Gate, Eye-Gate, Mouth-Gate, Nose-Gate and Feel-Gate—representing, of course, the senses. When Emmanuel's forces come to capture Mansoul they direct their attack first upon Ear-Gate. But Diabolus had taken his precautions to meet it, for he had stationed at Ear-Gate, says Bunyan, "one old Mr. Prejudice, an angry and ill-conditioned fellow, and put under his power sixty men, called deaf men—men advantageous for that service forasmuch as they mattered no words of the captains nor of the soldiers." Which being interpreted means that men's ears are closed against the Gospel by *prejudice.*

It was so more than nineteen hundred years ago in the case of the great man of the Jewish nation. It was prejudice that caused them to see no beauty in Christ that they should desire Him. It was prejudice that made them deaf to His appeals. It was prejudice that made them blind to His Divine majesty and power. It was prejudice that made them utterly reject His claims. "Search and look," they said in scornful tones, "for out of Galilee ariseth no prophet." Yes, old Mr. Prejudice, "that angry and ill-conditioned fellow," defended Ear-Gate nineteen hundred years ago only too well, so that instead of receiving Christ the Jews rejected Him and nailed Him to the tree.

Still today old angry and ill-conditioned Mr. Prejudice is doing his terrible work. I will not speak of the havoc he causes in daily life, half the unhappiness and injustice and unfairness of which is due to him. I will only speak of the way in which he and his deaf men still guard Ear-Gate against the appeals and calls of Emmanuel. Yes, I will venture to say that thousands and tens of thousands of people are being kept away from Christ by *prejudice.*

Some have been prejudiced against Him by what they see of Christian people; and some have been prejudiced against Him by the dogmas under which theologians have buried Him; and some have been prejudiced against Him by what sceptics have written about Him. They have taken their ideas of Christ from the imperfections of Christians, from the discussions of theologians, from the writings of unbelievers, and they have formed a prejudice against Him, and so have never come to the Christ Himself.

A caricature Christ prevents them from coming to the real Christ. That is the case with thousands of men and women today. It has been the case with men and women down through the centuries; it was very nearly the case with Nathanael long ago. "We have found Him of whom Moses in the Law and the Prophets did write, Jesus of Narazeth, the Son of Joseph," said his friend. And at the mention of Nazareth all Nathanael's prejudices were up in arms. "Can any good thing," he asked, "come out of Nazareth?" And when I read this I feel that instead of being one of the twelve, he might have been one of those who nailed Christ to the tree, but for one thing: with all his prejudices, Nathanael was a man of open and candid mind.

Nathanael, the Man without Guile

His preconceived ideas were his peril—his open and candid mind
was his salvation. "Can any good thing come out of Nazareth?" he
asked incredulously, in answer to Philip's announcement. And Philip,
instead of trying to argue or discuss the point, said to him, "Come and
see." To his everlasting credit and to his eternal salvation, Nathanael
went and saw. His countrymen, steeped in prejudice, refused to come
and see; they refused to examine and consider Christ's claims. But
Nathanael, though brought up in the same beliefs, yet possessed an
open and a candid mind, and so in answer to Philip's appeal he went
and saw, to the salvation of his soul.

In this fact you have the salient feature in Nathanael's character.
Our Lord Himself has pointed it out. "Behold," He said, as He saw
Nathanael approaching, "Behold an Israelite indeed, in whom is no
guile." Yes, that was Nathanael—he was a man without guile.

He was like the patriarch Jacob, a very prince with God in the
power of his prayers, but, unlike Jacob, he had not a trace of cunning
or deceit in his nature. Newman, in his second volume of *Sermons*,
says that the "guileless man" is described for us in the fifteenth Psalm.
Then David asks the question: "Lord, who shall sojourn in Thy Tab-
ernacle? Who shall dwell in Thy holy hill? He that walketh uprightly
and worketh righteousness and speaketh truth in his heart. He that
slandereth not with his tongue, nor doeth evil to his friend, nor
taketh up a reproach against his neighbor. He that sweareth to his
own hurt and changeth not." That is the picture of Nathanael.

Nathanael was the kind of man whom people say they can read
like a book. There was not a shred of trickery or duplicity about
Nathanael. He was absolutely transparent, single, sincere. They used
to say of him in the neighborhood that he would never make a
successful businessman. He was so confiding, so absolutely trustful.
He credited everyone with his own sincerity, with the result that he
was imposed upon again and again. Indeed, the sharp and not too
scrupulous traders of Galilee used to speak of Nathanael as being a bit
"simple." In Heaven's sight, however, Nathanael had chosen the
better part; the traders had chosen wealth, but he had chosen to keep
a good and honest soul.

"Guilelessness" is as much a discredited virtue here in the twenti-
eth century as it was in Galilee in the first. The very term breathes of

a contemptuous pity. When we say, "So-and-so is a guileless sort of
person," we do not mean it as a compliment. No, guilelessness is at a
discount among us. We pride ourselves upon being keen, well versed
in all the clever ways of business, acquainted with the tricks of every
trade. We glory today not in being guileless, but in being "smart."
And yet I had rather die a pauper and have written on my gravestone
this verse, "Behold an Israelite indeed, in whom is no guile," than I
would to have a millionaire's millions at the price of my honesty and
simplicity of soul.

Can this be said of us—that we are without guile? Is this the
character we bear in the world—that we are absolutely sincere and
single and transparent? Is that the reputation you businessmen have?
They tell me business is honeycombed with trickery and fraud. Have
we acquiesced in it on the ground that it is the custom of business?
We had better far know nothing of its tricks or its deceit, and just do
the honest and straightforward thing.

But, some may object, a person can never make money that way!
Note this well, it is not absolutely necessary that you should make
money, but it *is* necessary you should be honest. If men will call you
"innocent"—take it as a compliment. An honest heart, a guileless
soul, is more precious than rubies, and all the things you can desire
are not to be compared with it.

The Regard of the Guileless Heart

"Blessed are the pure in heart," said our Lord, "for they shall see
God." Nathanael would never have made a fortune at his business—
if you like so to put it. He was too innocent and confiding a soul. But
he had his rich reward—he saw God. Yes, this Israelite indeed, in
whom was no guile, found his King and his God in Jesus Christ. It
was this guileless man who made the fullest confession of faith in
Christ.

Nathanael realized more of the glory of Christ than anyone of his
fellow-disciples. In Christ Andrew found the Messiah. Philip found
in Christ, Him of whom Moses in the Law and the prophets did
write. But this man of the guileless soul saw more of the Divine glory
than anyone of them, and he made the great confession, "Thou art
the Son of God, Thou art King of Israel."

Though he was poor in this world's goods, Nathanael received the blessing of a vision of God. "I thank Thee, O Father, Lord of heaven and earth," said Jesus, "that Thou hast hid these things from the wise and prudent and didst reveal them unto babes." The condition of knowledge and vision in Divine things is the child heart, the innocent and guileless soul. That vision is the *summum bonum*. There is no good beyond it. It will profit us nothing though we gain the world, if we lose the vision. Therefore keep innocency, and do the thing which is right; keep a simple, honest, pure heart, and to you shall be given the supremest blessing of beholding with open face the glory of the Lord.

8

MATTHEW

"As Jesus went on from there, he saw a man named Matthew, sitting at the tax collector's booth; Follow me, he told him, and Matthew got up and followed him." —*Matthew 9:9 NIV*

IN JOHN HENRY NEWMAN'S second volume of *Parochial and Plain Sermons*, you will find a sermon for St. Matthew's Day called "The Danger of Riches." At first I wondered why that great preacher and keen student of human nature had chosen such a subject as being specially suitable for the day set apart to commemorate St. Matthew.

Had Newman made Judas his text for a sermon on the danger of riches, one could have seen the reason at once, for the story of Judas is the most tragic and appalling illustration in the world of the fatal effects of love of money. Judas bare the bag, and, according to the reiterated testimony of Scripture, it was his love of money that made him first a thief and finally a traitor.

But I could not at first understand why Matthew had been made the text for a sermon on the danger of riches, for I could not find a single sentence in the whole of Scripture definitely laying this sin of loving money to the charge of the seventh Apostle. Further consideration, however, convinced me that Newman's incomparable insight had not failed him here, but that in selecting "The Danger of Riches" as the solemn truth, and illustrated by the Apostle's career, he had, with his usual unerring instinct, fastened upon Matthew's besetting weakness and sin. Yes, there can be no doubt about it—Matthew loved money. His well-nigh fatal passion was love of money. Mat-

thew would have money—I was almost going to say at any price—
and for money's sake he all but—yes, he all but made his bed in hell.

Matthew's Love of Money

My justification for saying these strong things about Matthew and
his love of money is to be found in this one fact, that he was a
publican. Matthew's love of money must have become a consuming
and absorbing passion with him, or he would never have become a
publican. It must have come to this with him, that he was resolved to
make money anyhow—by fair means or foul—or he would never
have become a publican.

To become a publican in Palestine nineteen centuries ago a man
had first of all to sell his *country*. The publican was the servant and
agent of that mighty Rome which had robbed the Jews of their
freedom and planted its iron heel upon their necks. He was the
embodiment and representative of the foreign tyrant. For a Jew to
become a tax gatherer, to wear the Roman uniform, to become the
hireling of the Roman Government, was to commit the great aposta-
sy; it was to sin against that glorious blessed future foretold for the
Jewish nation by seer and Psalmist; it was to become the tool of the
oppressor.

Dr. Samuel Johnson once defined a pensioner as a State hireling
paid to betray his country. The Jew would have accepted that as a
true definition of the publican. He was a man who, attracted by the
gleam of Roman gold, turned renegade and traitor to his native land.

To become a publican, in the second place, a man had to sell his
conscience. The publican's trade was a dishonest one. The fact that
once in the history of the Empire a monument was raised to the
memory of a man whose chief distinction it was that he had been an
honest publican, only confirms the truth of the statement that, speaking generally, the publicans were a set of unscrupulous extortioners
and thieves.

Taxes today are usually fixed by responsible and representative
bodies, and the tax gatherer, as a result, can never exact more than is
due. But taxes long ago were "farmed." The taxes of a town or district
or province would be sold to the highest bidder, and that highest
bidder was then allowed to squeeze out of the people of his district
what money he could. It was a system that encouraged corruption

and extortion. The more the publican squeezed out of the people, the quicker he grew rich. And so the publican lied and cheated and swindled; he smothered his conscience and hardened his heart, and grew fat and rich by extortion and false accusation.

Matthew was a *publican*. I know not how soon the desire for money entered Matthew's soul, but before very long it had accomplished its fatal work there. For, as Newman says in that so searching sermon of his, the danger of *desiring* money is that the pursuit of money should become the end and aim of life. I do not know when Matthew had begun to desire money. This I do know, however. When Matthew had reached manhood, money had become the end and aim of his life. Yes, Matthew would have money at all costs—he would have it clean or unclean; and as the quickest and easiest way of making money was to become one of Caesar's tax gatherers, Matthew entered the detested service and became a Customs officer in Capernaum.

"The love of money," says the Apostle Paul, "is a root of all kinds of evil," and for illustration and proof of that saying I would quote Matthew's history. The love of money was the root of all kinds of evil in Matthew's case. For love of money he sold his country; for love of money he sold his conscience; for love of money he bargained away his spiritual privileges; for love of money he became an outcast and an alien from the commonwealth of Israel. Home, friends, conscience, religion—Matthew sacrificed them all on the altar of Mammon.

"They that desire to be rich," says the same Evangelical Apostle in the same letter, "fall into a temptation and a snare, and many foolish and hurtful lusts such as drown men in destruction and perdition." Matthew discovered that to his bitter cost. He had salved his conscience when he first took up with his hateful business by saying he would be an honest publican. But his desire to be rich soon proved too much for his honesty. He quickly fell in with the ways of his detestable business. "I must conform to custom," he said to his soul in self-excuse.

Thus it came to pass that in a very few months Matthew could cheat and lie and rob with the very best. In his desire for gold he stopped at nothing. He closed his ears against the cry of the widow and orphan; he hardened his heart against the appeals of the poor, he became a stranger to compassion and mercy. Yes, to such a pitch did Matthew's passion for wealth attain that, had not Jesus summoned him from that terrible toll booth, Matthew would not have had a shred of heart or conscience left, but he would have been utterly and forever drowned in destruction and perdition.

The Danger of Riches

Thus with this man Matthew as my text and illustration, I could, like Newman, preach a sermon on "The Danger of Riches," and in preaching such a sermon I should be preaching to the times. The longer I live the more convinced I become that there are statements in the Bible which we refuse to take seriously. And among such statements the most notable are those with reference to the perils of wealth. Yes, I will dare to say that there are no verses in the whole of the Bible so ignored, so deliberately set aside and flouted, as those which speak of the dangers of money.

You readers would be indignant with me if I said you did not believe what your Bibles say; and yet my experience of life convinces me that there are thousands and tens of thousands who disbelieve what the Bible says about riches. How otherwise can you account for the fact that they strain every nerve to acquire that very thing whose possession is so perilous to the soul?

Do you think people would strive for gold as they do if they honestly believed that the love of money is a root of all kinds of evil? Do you think they would struggle to get rich as they do if they honestly believed it was difficult for a rich man to enter the Kingdom of God? No, they would not. They are only able to live as they do because they disbelieve and set aside and explain away what the Bible says about wealth.

Yet, if there are any warnings in the old Book verified and emphasized by life and experience, they are the warnings it utters about the love of money. "They that desire to be rich fall into a temptation and a snare, and many foolish and hurtful lusts such as drown men in destruction and perdition"—it is as true today as it was twenty centuries ago. Love of money is the root of all kinds of evil. Lust and drink slay their thousands, but greed slays its tens of thousands.

Mammon is God's greatest rival in the world today. The possession of wealth materializes the soul, so that people begin to feel they are rich and increased with goods and in need of nothing. The desire for wealth makes people willing to sacrifice honor and conscience.

Matthew knew by bitter experience the fatal and blighting effect of this love of money, for he himself had been all but drowned in perdition and destruction on account of it. It would be salvation to the business and professional people of the world if they would but read the verses about wealth which Matthew has preserved for us in his Gospel, emphasized and underlined as they are by Matthew's terrible experience. Yes, it would be for the eternal profit of people of business if they prepared for work each day by writing on their hearts these words from Matthew's Gospel: "Lay not up for yourselves treasures upon the earth, where moth and rust doth consume, and where thieves break through and steal; but lay up for yourselves treasures in Heaven, where neither moth nor rust doth consume, and where thieves do not break through nor steal."

Remember, Jesus also said: "Be not anxious for your life what ye shall eat or what ye shall drink, nor yet for your body what ye shall put on." "What is a man profited, if he shall gain the whole world and lose his own soul, or what shall a man give in exchange for his soul?" And, finally, this terrible passage: "Again I say unto you, It is easier for a camel to go through the eye of a needle, than for a rich man to enter the Kingdom of God."

Matthew the Publican

Matthew's soul might have been utterly drowned in destruction and perdition in that toll booth of his had not Jesus visited Capernaum. All Galilee rang with the fame of the Prophet from Nazareth, and wherever He went there was great curiosity to see and hear Him. The excitement spread even to those who never frequented the meetings of the synagogue. "The publicans and sinners gathered themselves together to hear Him." And among the publicans who heard Jesus preach His first sermon in Capernaum was Matthew. It was curiosity that brought Matthew to hear the sermon, but the sermon he heard proved to be the turning point in his life. Matthew had never heard preaching like this before. As he stood and listened, it seemed as if the Preacher were preaching directly to him. Yes, it seemed to Matthew as if the Preacher knew all about him, and was just speaking to him alone.

Those clear eyes searched him through and through, and the words He spoke probed his very soul. "No man," said the Preacher, looking Matthew full in the face, "no man can serve two masters, for either he will hate the one and love the other, or else he will hold to one and despise the other. Ye cannot serve God and Mammon." And again, "Seek ye first the Kingdom of God and His righteousness, and all these things shall be added unto you." And again this, "Whosoever would save his life shall lose it, and whosoever shall lose his life for My sake shall find it."

Matthew went back to his toll booth when the sermon was done, but he could not forget the Preacher and those clear eyes and searching words. Christ's sermon that day brought Matthew's conscience back to life again, so that of all those in Capernaum there was none more wretched and miserable than he. He tried to banish the Preacher and His sermon from his thoughts by plunging more fiercely than ever into business, but it was all in vain. The sermon would not be banished. Wherever he looked—in his ledgers and his accounts, on his office walls—he seemed to behold this sentence, "Ye cannot serve God and Mammon." Through every conversation this one sentence rang in his ear, "Ye cannot serve God and Mammon," until poor Matthew became completely distracted, and his toll booth a veritable place of torment to him.

I do not know how it would all have ended had not Jesus presented Himself at the booth one day and said to the well-nigh demented Matthew in a tone of regal command, "Follow Me. Leave this hateful and destroying toll booth, and follow Me." It was the call Matthew longed to hear, and he instantly obeyed it. Yes, Matthew stepped out of his toll booth and stepped into liberty and Peace. "He arose and followed Him." And thus it came to pass that Jesus had a publican among the chosen twelve.

Our Lord showed a magnificent disregard of the dictates of worldly wisdom in His choice of Apostles. "Ye see your calling, brethren," says Paul in his letter to the Corinthians, "how that not many wise men after the flesh, not many mighty, not many noble are called." In this list of twelve there is not one rich man, there is not one of noble birth, there is not one of University education. For the first teachers of the new faith Christ chose the foolish things and the weak things and the things that are despised of the world, in the persons of Peter and James, and John and Andrew, and Philip and Thomas—humble, unlettered peasants and fishermen of Galilee. But if Jesus showed a disregard of worldly wisdom in His choice of Peter and James and John and the rest, in His choice of Matthew He set every consideration of worldly prudence aside. I say, when Jesus, in the eye of day and in the full sight of men, went up to Matthew in his detested toll booth and said to him, "Follow Me," and gave to this loathed and hated publican a place in His Apostolate, He flew in the face of worldly wisdom.

It shocked all Palestine, and especially religious Palestine, to see an outcast publican amongst the chosen intimates of Christ. It shocked Palestine, I say; but for nearly twenty centuries now it has been bringing hope and courage to a sin-stricken and almost despairing world.

Yes, I never read in the list of the twelve the name of *Matthew the publican* without thanking God and taking courage. I rejoice to find the name of the impulsive and enthusiastic Peter amongst the twelve. I rejoice to find the name of the fearless and intrepid James amongst the twelve. I rejoice to find the name of the seraphic and warmhearted John amongst the twelve. I rejoice to find the name of the humble and faithful Andrew and the seeking Philip and the guileless Bartholomew among the twelve. But as a sin-burdened and guilty sinner, I rejoice most of all to find amongst the twelve the name of Matthew the publican. For the name of Matthew in this list is evidence to me of the saving power of Jesus Christ; it is proof to me "that sinners Jesus will receive" and that therefore there is hope for me—even me.

There are some wonderful verses in the old Book about the freeness and universality of the Gospel welcome, verses that seem at times almost too good to be true. But I find myself able to believe them all when I see Matthew the publican's name in the list of the twelve. I read that word of Jesus, "The Son of Man is come to seek and to save that which is lost," and I can believe it, for I see Matthew's name in the list of the twelve. I read that other word of our Lord's, "Him that cometh to Me I will in no wise cast out," and I can believe it, for I see Matthew's name in the list of the twelve. In the Epistle to the Hebrews I read that "He is able to save them to the uttermost that come unto God by Him," and I can believe there is none beyond the reach of His saving arm, for I see the name of Matthew the publican in the list of the twelve. And I read in the last chapter of the old Book, and almost in its last verses, that unrestricted and pressing invitation, "The Spirit and the Bride say, Come. And let him that heareth say, Come. And let him that is athirst, come. And whosoever will, let him take the water of life freely."

And I can believe that *whosoever will* may come, for I see the name of Matthew the publican in the list of the twelve. And with Matthew the publican as my text, I will preach the glad gospel of a universal welcome and an uttermost salvation. Yes, whosoever will may come; and no matter how sinful a man may be, Jesus can save. There is not one in the wide world today outside the welcome of that love that welcomed Matthew; and there is not one in the wide world today beyond the reach of that Arm that rescued and saved Matthew. The Jesus who turned Matthew the publican into Matthew the Apostle can take the vilest and guiltiest of us and set us among princes and make us inherit a throne of glory.

Matthew's Feast

The first service that Matthew the redeemed publican did for Jesus his Redeemer was to make Him a great feast. Of all the feasts that ever Jesus attended, I question whether there was one so completely to His heart as the one Matthew made for Him that day. For the feast was the offering of a grateful soul, and the company was of the kind that Jesus loved to meet. This is Luke's account of that never-to-be forgotten feast: "And Levi made him a great feast in his house; and there was a great multitude of publicans and of others that were sitting at meat with them." About this feast I could say much did time permit, for it is full of deep and beautiful significance. But I will confine myself to making two remarks about it.

(1) This feast was Matthew's testimony to his own *gladness of heart.* Men have the notion that the service of Christ means deprivation and loss and bondage. Matthew's great feast testifies that to him at least Christ's service was *perfect freedom.* Matthew had been kicking against the pricks in the toll booth. Yes, for a long time he had been fighting with his inner self. His conscience gave him no peace nor rest. He grew to hate his odious trade even while he clung to it; so that, as I have said, all Capernaum did not contain a more miserable and unhappy man than Matthew the publican in his toll booth. So when Jesus came and ordered him out of it, it was a veritable deliverance to Matthew.

Yes, it was an emancipation from worse than Egyptian bondage to Matthew. It is true he sacrificed his hope of fortune when he left the toll booth. But the peace that came to his soul was worth ten thousand fortunes. This feast was the captive's rejoicing over his new-gained liberty. It was the slave's thanksgiving for the breaking of his bonds. It was Matthew's way of testifying to his new-found joy, of declaring what great things God had done for his soul. As Dr. A. B. Bruce puts it, this feast was a kind of poem, Matthew saying in act what Doddridge has said in verse—

> *Oh, happy day that fixed my choice*
> *On Thee, my Savior and my God.*

(2) Secondly, this feast was Matthew's plan of *introducing his Savior to others of his old associates who needed salvation*. In speaking of the Apostles who have already passed under our notice, I have had occasion to call attention to the fact that as soon as ever they discovered in Christ the Redeemer of their souls, they were anxious to impart their glad discovery to others.

Andrew went straight from his first interview with Jesus and told his brother Peter, "We have found Messiah." John, I well believe, went straight from that same interview to tell his brother James. Philip had no sooner received the good news into his own heart than he must hurry off to impart it to Nathanael, his friend under the fig tree.

The word burned like a fire in the bones of these men, and they had to speak it. It was a day of good tidings, and they felt constrained to tell. And so exactly Matthew, as soon as he had been delivered from that hell of a toll booth and brought forth into the liberty and peace of the children of God, wanted to tell his brother publicans of his Redeemer. He knew there were multitudes of men working for the Romans just as unhappy and as utterly desperate as he was. And he wanted to bring them to the great Physician of Souls, who could do as much for them as He had done for him.

That is why Matthew sent invitations to all the publicans of the town and district to come to dine at his house and meet Jesus. There was scarcely one who declined the invitation. "There was a great company"—"multitude," the Revised Version has it—"there was a great multitude of publicans and of others who sat at meat with them." To these stricken and outcast souls the Lord Jesus spoke comfortable words—and of Matthew's house and Matthew's feast it will be declared in the great day—that this and that soul was born there.

Thus, Matthew's first deed as a Christian disciple was to bring other sin-sick souls to Jesus. Let me press the question upon you once again. Have you ever introduced anyone to Jesus? Have you ever made a great feast in His honor, and have you ever invited friends and associates to meet Him? Have you ever so felt the unspeakable preciousness of your own redemption that you have felt constrained to tell others of it? Redeemed yourself, have you ever become a preacher of redemption?

There is a world around us lying in darkness and in sin; have you ever gone forth to tell anyone in it about the Savior? When Rabbi Duncan, the great Presbyterian professor of Hebrew, was dying in Edinburgh, someone told him there was a man in the infirmary whose language no one could speak. "I will learn it, I will learn it," said the dying scholar, "that I may tell him about the Savior." Have you ever felt a passion like that—a passionate longing to tell every sinner you meet about the Savior? We will not have to wait long for the conversion of the world once Christian people feel like Paul, "Woe is me if I preach not the Gospel," and begin boldly and joyfully to declare to all with whom they come in contact God's righteousness and God's salvation.

"When Matthew rose up and left all and followed our Lord," says Dr. Alexander Whyte, "the only thing he took with him out of his old occupation was his pen and ink." With his pen and ink he wrote for us the glorious Gospel that bears his name. He himself disappears from the history after the record of his great feast. But by the Gospel he wrote he still continued to comfort and gladden the souls of men.

In like manner we, though we be too humble for our names to appear in any history, may become Epistles of Christ written not with ink, but with the spirit of the living God; not in tables of stone, but in tables that are hearts of flesh, and may shine as lights in the world, holding forth the word of life.

9

THOMAS

"Then Thomas (called Didymus) said to the rest of the disciples,
'Let us also go, that we may die with him.'" —John 11:16 NIV

THE OLD PHYSIOLOGISTS used to say that there were four human
temperaments: the sanguine, the phlegmatic, the choleric, and the
melancholic. Each of these temperaments, I have imagined, had its
representative or representatives in the circle of the twelve. The
sanguine temperament had its representative in the prince and primate
of the twelve—the impetuous and enthusiastic Peter. The phlegmatic
temperament had its representative in the slow but practical Philip.
The choleric temperament had its representatives in those two fiery
souls James and John, the Sons of Thunder. And, without doubt, the
melancholic temperament had its representative in the person of
Thomas, who is also called Didymus. That is really the key to Thomas'
character. He was a melancholy man.

"If to say man is to say melancholy," says Dr. Alexander Whyte, of
Edinburgh, "then to say Thomas, who is also called Didymus, is to say
religious melancholy." "Man is born to trouble as the sparks fly up-
ward," says the old Book. Not a man passes through life without
having his times of grief, his days when the sun withdraws itself and
there is not a star to be seen in his sky. Not a man makes the
pilgrimage of life but at one stage or another he is led into some
valley of weeping.

But there are some poor souls whose *whole* time seems to be spent
in grief, whose *every* day is a day of gloom, and who seem not so

95

much to *pass through* the Valley of Baca as to make it their perpetual abode. There are some unhappy people who seem constitutionally unable to smile. They were born sad. Their hearts are the homes of a constant sorrow. They can never see the sun for the cloud. They are dull, not to say blind, to the bright side of life, but keenly sensitive to its woe and its pain. The great but gloomy English moralist, Samuel Johnson, was one of these. "Poor Johnson," as Carlyle says, "had to go about girt with continual hypochondria, physical and spiritual pain. Like a Hercules with the burning Nessus shirt on him, which shoots in on him dull, incurable misery—the Nessus shirt, not to be stripped off, which is his own natural skin." And Thomas, who is called Didymus, was another of that unhappy and much afflicted company. Thomas looked upon life with sad eyes. He carried about with him everywhere a heavy heart. He was a melancholy man.

Thomas and Mr. Fearing

John Bunyan, that inimitable artist and delineator of human character, has given us in his *Pilgrim* a series of immortal portraits, and among the rest he has given us the portrait of the melancholy Thomas. Yes, Thomas sat for his portrait to the dreamer of Bedford, and the result is the character of Mr. Fearing. In him we have the melancholy Apostle's picture drawn to the very life. You perhaps remember Great Heart's description of Mr. Fearing. "He was a man of choice spirit," said this valiant champion in his conversation with that notable pilgrim Old Honest, "only he was always kept very low, and that made his life so burdensome to himself and so troublesome to others."

"But what," asked that worthy old gentleman, "should be the reason that such a good man should be all his days so much in the dark?"

"There are two reasons for it," answered Great Heart. "One is, the wise God will have it so; some men must pipe and some must weep. Now, Mr. Fearing was one that played upon this Base; he and his fellows sound the sackbut whose notes are more doleful than the notes of other musick are, though indeed some say the Base is the ground of music. The first string that the musician usually touches is the Bass, when he intends to put all in tune. Only here was the imperfection of Mr. Fearing, he could play upon no other musick, but this, till toward his latter end."

Yes, without doubt that is Thomas to the very life. As John Bunyan says, in his own quaint way, "He was one of those that played upon the Bass; if there was a doleful, dismal, sombre note to be struck you could depend upon Thomas to strike it." Others might play upon the more cheerful pipe and cornet and organ, but Thomas could play upon no other music but this bass of his—at any rate, not until the end of the days of his discipleship and the appearance to him of the risen Lord.

"He was a man of choice spirit, only he was always kept very low," and in that one sentence Bunyan has so summed up Thomas' character that it is impossible to add to it or improve upon it. Our very best and greatest scholars have tried to characterize Thomas for us. "A man of much love and little faith," is Westcott's description of him. "He was a man of candor and resolution, but inclined to subordinate the invisible to the visible," says Godet. "A man of warm heart but of melancholy temperament," says Dr. A. B. Bruce. But the tinker's picture is the best and truest of them all; this is the Thomas revealed to us in the Gospels: "He was a man of choice spirit, only he was always kept very low."

Thomas' Devotion

That is the first remark I would like to make about Thomas—he was *a man of choice spirit.* He must have been that, or he would never have been among the twelve. It was not for his melancholy Christ called him—Christ called him because He saw him to be a man of choice spirit. Thomas has never yet had justice done to him by the Christian Church. The nobility and worth of his character have never been fairly recognized. Thomas has come down the centuries with a nickname attached to him. By sheer force of custom, Thomas has come to be so associated and identified with his nickname, that whenever we mention him we instinctively add his nickname and speak of him as Thomas *the Doubter!*

Everything else about Thomas has been lost sight of and forgotten in his *doubt.* But that is to do a grievous wrong to Thomas. For *doubt* was not his chief characteristic. Thomas' chief characteristic was *a deep and devoted love.* Yes, I would have you know that Thomas, to use John Bunyan's words, was a man of *choice spirit.* Of all His disciples, Christ had none more devoted, more whole-souled, more enthusiastic than this man Thomas. Thomas left all for Christ. Thomas dared all for Christ. Thomas was ready to die for Christ. The deepest thing in Thomas, I repeat, was not his *doubt*, but his *unquenchable love* for Jesus Christ. If you want evidence of Thomas' devoted love you cannot do better than refer to the incident from the account of which my text is taken. To escape the murderous hate of the Jews, Jesus had withdrawn into Perea. While He was there the sisters of Bethany sent a message to Him, saying, "He whom Thou lovest is sick." It was a tacit appeal, "Come over and help us." Jesus did not all at once respond to the appeal, but at the end of two days He said to His disciples, "Let us go into Judaea again."

To the disciples the suggestion seemed sheer madness. "Rabbi," they said protestingly, "the Jews were but now seeking to stone Thee, and goest Thou thither again?" To venture into Judea seemed to these disciples equivalent to rushing upon certain destruction, and they were afraid to venture.

I wonder if these timid and frightened men might have anticipated the shame of the garden and forsaken Christ there and then in Perea had it not been for Thomas. The one man of heroic spirit amongst them that day was Thomas; the one man out of whose heart perfect love had wholly cast forth fear was Thomas; the one man to speak brave words of loyalty and unfaltering fidelity was Thomas. "Let us also go," said he to these fainting and halting disciples, "let us also go, that we may die with Him."

Like the rest, Thomas anticipated the very worst result of the journey. He could see nothing but death as the inevitable end of the venture. Yet come what might he was resolved never to leave Jesus Christ. Yes, Thomas was willing to face the most cruel of deaths for Jesus Christ.

"Let us also go," said this man of choice spirit and of devoted heart, "that we may die with Him." Like those knights in attendance upon the blind King John of Bohemia, who rode into the battle of Crecy with their bridles intertwined with that of their master, resolved to share his fate whatever it might be—so Thomas, come life, come death, was resolved never to forsake his Lord, bound as he was to Him by a bond of deep and enthusiastic love.

"He was a man of choice spirit." Yes, for devotion and heroic love I know of no one to excel Thomas. "As the Lord liveth," said Elisha in answer to Elijah's appeal to him to leave him, "as the Lord liveth and as thy soul liveth, I will not leave thee."

"Entreat me not to leave thee," said Ruth, the Moabitess, to Naomi her mother-in-law; "whither thou goest I will go; where thou lodgest I will lodge; where thou diest I will die, and there will I be buried; the Lord do so to me and more also if aught but death part thee and me."

Those are moving and pathetic instances of loyalty, but they are not more moving and pathetic than the loyalty with which Thomas was ready to dare anything for his Master. "Let us also go," said this man of the devoted heart, "that we may die with Him."

As it is Thomas' chief characteristic, it is also his crowning glory. Of Thomas it might be said, as of the woman who was much forgiven, that "he loved much." He loved Christ with all the fervor and passion of his deep and sorrowful heart. And here I hold out Thomas—this so passionate lover of Jesus—for your admiration and imitation. Thomas had his weaknesses and failings, but he also had that supreme virtue, that most excellent grace which covers a multitude of sins and makes a man a Christian indeed—he loved his Master with an unfeigned, enthusiastic, whole-hearted love.

Do you have Thomas' devoted and consecrated heart? Have you Thomas' passionate and heroic love? It would be easy to excel Thomas in the things of the intellect (the brain). It would be easy to excel him in the understanding of mysteries and of knowledge. But of what avail are these without love? "Though I have the gift of prophecy," says the most evangelical of the Apostles, "and know all mysteries and all knowledge, and though I have all faith so as to remove mountains and have not *love*, I am nothing."

It is love Christ wants. It is the offering of a consecrated heart He desires. And I put the question to you now: Do you have Thomas' love? Have you given your Lord an undivided heart? Do you love Him so well that you feel you can dare all and suffer all for His sake?

How many of us love Christ so well that we can say with Thomas, "Let us also go with Him, that *we may die with Him*"? How many of us can say that? It is a searching test; but let us honestly try ourselves by it, for there is a terrible word in the old Book which says that unless a man hates father and mother and wife and child—yea, and *his own life also,* he cannot be Christ's disciple. Tried by that test I do not know how many disciples Christ has in the world; but this I know, that, in view of this terrible word, there is no prayer we need more to offer than an earnest and importunate prayer to be given Thomas' heart, a heart consumed and possessed with a passionate love for Christ. With that kind of love we may be able to take those words of absolute and burning devotion into our life, and say—

> *If Jesus Christ is a man,*
> *And only a man, I say*
> *That of all mankind I will cleave to Him,*
> *And to Him will I cleave alway.*

> *If Jesus Christ is a God,*
> *And the only God, I swear*
> *I will follow Him through heaven and hell,*
> *The earth, the sea and the air.*

Thomas' Depression

"He was a man of choice spirit," says Bunyan of Mr. Fearing, "only he was always kept very low." And that is Thomas exactly. *He was always kept very low.* Thomas always saw the dark side of things. Invariably he took a gloomy view. His tune was always pitched in a minor key. He spent most of his time in the Valley of Humiliation or the Slough of Despond or the Dungeons of Doubting Castle, and so his life was burdensome to himself and troublesome to others.

In the first place, he was always kept *very low about his own spiritual condition.* "He was above many tender of Sin," says John Bunyan of Mr. Fearing. And that was also true of Thomas. He was very tender of sin. Not one in the whole group of the Apostolate had such a vivid sense of sin as Thomas had. Plagued by the corruption and depravity of his own heart, he looked within and abhorred himself. "Mine iniquities," he used to cry with the Psalmist, "have taken hold upon me so that I am not able to look up."

He spent his days in grief and his nights in sighing, and the cause of his grief and his sighing was his terrible sin. Thomas was indeed often tempted to doubt whether God would receive so vile and guilty a wretch as he. He was never one of those who contended who should be greatest. Thomas was never one of those to boast, "We have left all and followed Thee." Thomas always wondered how ever he came to be one of the twelve at all.

No, this is not imagination or fancy. I have Scriptural warrant for what I am saying. If you will turn to the Gospel lists you will find the names of Thomas and Matthew the publican coupled together. Thomas and Matthew were inseparables. Thomas clung to Matthew as his very shadow. Thomas never aspired to be among the first. Thomas chose for his friend and intimate Matthew the publican, the man who had fallen lowest of all the group. Why did he choose Matthew? He chose him just because he had been a publican—just because he had fallen so low into the horrible pit and the miry clay. Matthew brought hope to Thomas' sorrowful and melancholy heart. Yes, Matthew often came between Thomas and despair. For Matthew the publican was the living assurance of God's willingness to receive and Christ's power to save even to the uttermost. It was exactly characteristic of this man, who was always kept very low, that Matthew the publican should be his chosen friend.

And, secondly, Thomas was just as despondent *about his Master and his Master's Kingdom* as he was about himself. He is only mentioned three times in the Sacred Narrative, but each time he "plays upon his bass," and is kept very low. Even that incident in Perea which displayed his courage displayed also his gloominess and despondency. Thomas was quite sure that to return to Judea meant death to them all. In the Upper Room, when Jesus was talking to them about the Father's house and the Prepared Place, and taking it for granted that they knew where He was going and the way that led to it—it was Thomas who broke in with the sad and hopeless remark, "Lord, we know not whither Thou goest; how know we the way?"

But Thomas' melancholy reached its lowest depth on the evening of the third day after the Passion. When Thomas saw his Lord hanging on the tree, he fell into a perfect fit of despair. When the great stone was rolled on to the mouth of the tomb, the deep night settled down on Thomas' soul. For the Cross was the death-blow to every hope that Thomas had ever cherished in his gloomy heart.

Yes, it is no exaggeration to say that after the Crucifixion poor, melancholy Thomas lived in the "outer darkness," and walked about with a broken heart. Now, excessive grief is proverbially selfish. After he had seen his Lord die, Thomas had no pleasure in the company of his fellow-disciples. He would rather be alone, brooding over his great grief. And so it happened that when Jesus came on the evening of the first day in the week and stood in the midst of His disciples, Thomas was not with them. When, later, he returned, the disciples greeted him with the glad announcement, "We have seen the Lord."

Moody, melancholy, heart-broken Thomas could not and would not believe it. The news was too good to be true. "Except," he answered disconsolately, "except I shall see in His hand the print of the nails, and put my finger into the print of the nails, and put my hand into His side, I will not believe." And so Thomas, the man of melancholy, became Thomas the Doubter.

The Doubt of Thomas

When I come to deal with the doubt of Thomas, I am much tempted to criticize what many preachers and writers have said about it. For they have, to my mind, put wrong interpretations upon Thomas and his doubt—or what may be better termed his despair. But perhaps I will employ my time and yours better if, instead of criticizing what others have said, I state as briefly as I can two or three things that are obviously true about Thomas' despair.

1) First, then, the doubt or despair of Thomas sprang not from his *head*, but from his *heart*; it was the result not of intellectual difficulty, but of *great sorrow*. There is no analogy or kinship, therefore, between the doubt of Thomas and the speculative doubt of our own day, caused as that is by intellectual and philosophical difficulties. If you want to find the true analogy to this despair of Thomas, visit some home where "in the shadow of a great affliction, a soul sits dumb." Sorrow has the power for a time of separating men from God, of making faith falter, of bringing the horror of a great darkness into their sky.

I have seen husbands who have lost their wives, wives who have lost their husbands, parents who have lost their children. I have seen them in the very same plight as Thomas—unable to believe, unable to realize that Jesus was alive. I have letters in my desk just now such as Thomas might have written on any one of the ten days after the Passion. "I can see no gleam of light, and have lost my hold of God," writes one out of the midst of crushing grief. And that was exactly the case with Thomas. "Much learning hath made thee mad," said Sextus of Paul. And much grief had made Thomas a doubter, had made him lose his hold of God.

2) Thomas' doubt was one that made him *unutterably wretched*. I

question, indeed, whether Jerusalem contained a more miserable man than Thomas during those dark days before the second Sabbath. Thomas felt that, having lost his Lord, he had lost everything. And in this respect again Thomas' doubt differs from much of the doubt of the present day. For I will dare to say that much of the so-called doubt of the present day is flippant and thoughtless and assumed. Of all painful sights to be seen in this world, the most painful is that of the "flippant doubter."

"There are but two classes of men who can be called reasonable," says Pascal, "those who serve God with all their heart because they know Him, or those who seek for Him with their whole heart because they know Him not." And that great student of the human heart goes on to add, "I have nothing but compassion for all who sincerely lament their doubt, who look upon it as the worst of evils, and spare no pains to escape from it; but if this condition of doubt forms the subject of a man's joy and boasting, I have no terms in which to describe a creature so extravagant."

3) Thomas' doubt was the doubt of one who *wanted to believe*. He would have given anything to be really certain Jesus was alive. Yes, he would have given his very life for that happy assurance. He wanted to believe. Passionately he longed to come into touch with the living Lord.

In this respect again Thomas' doubt differed from much of the doubt of the present day. I do not want to say harsh things about the men and women of our time. I want to think the best and believe the best of them. Our sympathies have been claimed for the doubter, and I am ready to extend them heartily and freely to every doubter who agonizes over his doubt and longs for the light. But truth constrains me to say that nine out of ten of the doubters of the present day never agonize over their doubts. Their doubt is not born of difficulty and travail of soul.

I will be bold to say that most of those who pose as doubters do not believe because they do not *want* to believe. In a word, I am driven to the terrible conclusion that most of the "doubt" of the present day springs not from difficulties, but from *sin*. People are taken captive by the lusts of the flesh and the lusts of the eyes and the vainglory of life, and they cannot afford to believe. They seek to salve their souls and mollify their consciences by trying to persuade themselves that there is no God and no judgment, and no heaven and no hell. It is the doubt of people who do not want to believe.

That line of Tennyson has been quoted almost *ad nauseam*—

> *There lives more faith in honest doubt,*
> *Believe me, than in half the creeds.*

It has not only been quoted *ad nauseam* but it has been woefully abused. I will accept that couplet, however, if you will emphasize the word "honest." I am ready to believe that there is more faith in *"honest"* doubt than in half the creeds men repeat so easily and glibly. But, mind you, the doubt must be *honest.* I have no admiration to spare and I have no sympathy to waste upon the doubt borrowed from the pages of magazines; I have no pity for second-hand and borrowed skepticism; I have no compassion for doubt which has never cost the doubter a pang. But I have sympathy and pity for *honest* doubt.

The marks of *honest* doubt are these: first of all, it is an agony, and secondly, it pants and yearns and cries for the light. And further, I have this good news for the "honest" doubter—he will in time come to the light. "They that seek Me, shall find Me," says the old Book. To those who earnestly and sincerely desire to know Christ—Christ will show Himself.

Listen to Thomas' story: "After eight days again His disciples were within and Thomas with them. Jesus cometh, the doors being shut, and stood in the midst and said, Peace be unto you. Then saith He to Thomas, Reach hither thy finger and see My Hands; and reach hither thy hand and put it into My side, and be not faithless, but believing. Thomas answered and said unto Him, My Lord and my God."

Our Lord pitied this disciple of His, so unhappy in his doubt, so anxious to believe, and paid another visit for his special comfort. Then from the lips of Thomas the Doubter came the grandest expression of faith, "My Lord and my God." So to every anxious and seeking soul Christ will in due season reveal Himself, and doubt will end in happy faith.

"Those that seek Me, shall find Me." The man whose unbelief springs from an evil heart may remain forever in the dark, and upon them who at present sit in darkness but sigh and long for the day, the great light shall shine. There may be a troubled person reading this book. *Sursum corda.* Lift up your hearts:

> *"Wait thou His time—so shall thy night*
> *Soon end in perfect day."*

Only, in the meantime, do as Thomas did. Join with Christ's people, and cling to Christ even though to you He be but the man Jesus who lived and died nineteen centuries ago. Yes, cling to the Jesus you know; cherish Him in your heart, serve Him with your life, and you will soon know the living Christ. That is your present duty—cling to Him, obey Jesus, follow Jesus. I have a life in Christ to live, I have a death in Christ to die.

> *"And must I wait till science give*
> *All doubts a full reply?*
> *Nay, rather while the sea of doubt*
> *Is raging wildly round about,*
> *Questioning of life and death and sin,*
> *Let me but creep within*
> *Thy fold, O Christ, and at Thy feet*
> *Take but the lowest seat."*

He who does that will arrive some day at the haven of a quiet faith. To Him the Christ will reveal Himself, and like Thomas, he will say, "My Lord and my God."

10

SIMON THE ZEALOT

"Simon the Zealot."   —Matthew 10:4 NIV

"Simon, who was called the Zealot."   —Luke 6:15 NIV

LET ME BEGIN by correcting a misconception which I imagine is fairly general. The epithet "Cananite," which both Matthew and Mark (3:10) apply to this lesser known Simon, is *not* a geographical term. It has no connection whatever with the word "Canaan"—the alternative name for the country of Palestine. Nor does it contain any reference to the Galilean village of Cana, as Luther and Bengel seem to think. The epithet "Cananite" is derived from a Syriac word *Kanean* or *Kaneniah*, the name of a Jewish sect. It is, indeed, the exact Hebrew equivalent of that word ζηλωτής which we find in Luke's account, and the English word "zealot" fairly represents its meaning.

All that we know, therefore, of this Simon is summed up in the one word "Zealot." Unlike his great namesake, the prince and primate of the twelve, who figures so largely in the Gospels and the Book of the Acts of the Apostles, not a single word that this Simon ever said or a single deed he ever did has been recorded for us. This epithet "Zealot" is the only key we have to his character.

I have read of great zoologists like Sir Richard Owen, who from one bone have been able correctly to sketch the structure of animals long since extinct. But it is dangerous on the strength of one adjective to try to depict the character of a man. And yet the particular adjective here applied to Simon is so significant and involves so

107

much that the Apostle ceases to be a mere name, and we are able to recognize—at any rate in main outline—the manner of man he was. The late Dean Plumptre wrote in the early numbers of the *Expositor* what he called "ideal biographies" of the prophet Ezekiel and the writer of the Book of Ecclesiastes. He called them "ideal" biographies because, to a very large extent, they were works of imagination, and were not based upon definite and ascertained historic data. It would be relatively easy to write an "ideal biography" of this man Simon, and to make out of it an interesting and even romantic story. This would be all the easier because there is not a single fact of his personal history left on record. But it is not my desire or intention to weave out of my imagination a purely fancy sketch. I want to base myself upon the solid ground of *fact*. I want, as far as is possible, to get at the *real* Simon, and so I shall say nothing about Simon which is not justified by this epithet that is inseparable from his proper name.

Simon's Zeal

This is the first and most obvious thing that his soubriquet tells us about Simon. He was a man of *an ardent and enthusiastic spirit*. The various members of the Apostolic company were, as I have before said, distinguished for various qualities. There were "diversities of gifts." Peter was distinguished for his impetuosity and flashes of heaven by insight. James was distinguished for his superb and magnificent courage. John was distinguished for his seraphic love. Andrew was distinguished for his humility. Philip was distinguished for his practical common-sense. Bartholomew (or Nathanael) was distinguished for his child-like simplicity and devotion. Matthew was distinguished for his skill with the pen and the ink-horn. Thomas was distinguished for his moody but steadfast fidelity. But the mark of this Simon was his *burning and flaming zeal*. Yes, for ardor and enthusiasm the palm amongst the twelve had to be accorded to Simon, who was called the Zealot.

Judging from the position Simon's name occupies in the Apostolic list, and from the utter and absolute silence of Scripture with regard to any word or deed of his, I gather that Simon was in no sense a great, or gifted, or distinguished man. But he had that for lack of which great gifts often run to utter waste. He had an earnest and devoted soul. He had a fiery and unquenchable enthusiasm.

Yes, Christ had many a disciple more gifted, but He had none who served Him with a more perfect heart and with a more consuming ardor than this Simon who was called the Zealot. In his letter to the Galatians, Paul speaks about "the marks of the Lord Jesus." One of the marks of the Lord Jesus was a holy and untiring zeal. When His disciples noticed how intent He was from early morn till dewy eve upon His Father's business, to the utter disregard of His own personal comfort; when they saw Him neglecting His necessary food in His eagerness to minister to the sick and diseased and broken-hearted, they were reminded of that old verse which says: "The zeal of thine house hath eaten me up."

Simon bore upon himself this mark of the Lord Jesus. He was a man of boundless and tireless zeal. "He was a whole man to one thing at once," it was said of Sir Walter Raleigh. "He was a whole man to one thing *all the time*," it might have been said of Simon. Simon had but one object in life. He had but one interest. To that one object and interest he bent his every energy. "This one thing I do," he might have cried with the Apostle Paul, "I serve Christ and preach the kingdom." To that blessed work Simon devoted himself body, soul and spirit. He was at it in season and out, pursuing it with a quenchless and indomitable enthusiasm. Other Apostles, I repeat, excelled him in gifts and genius, but for holy zeal there was none more like the Lord than Simon the Zealot.

Zeal may be misdirected, but zeal in itself is a most blessed grace. I know of nothing we need more at this time than a quickening and renewal of *our zeal*. The Church needs the Zealot. Turn your eyes and glance backwards over the history of the Church, and you will find that her great days have been days when there were zealots in her midst. The flame of religious revival is always kindled at the zealot's heart. Italy leaped into new religious life under the preaching of a zealot named Francis of Assisi. The frivolous and dissipated Florence became for a season the city of the Great King under the preaching of a zealot in the person of the great Reformer, Girolamo Savonarola.

Eighteenth century England sunk in ignorance, immorality and sin, was quickened into new life under the preaching of two flaming zealots named John Wesley and George Whitefield. Another great evangelistic force in England came in the person of another zealot—fanatic, some people would call him—William Booth, of the Salvation Army.

We are *sorely in need of the zealot in these days*. These days are great days in many respects; they are great days so far as the achievements of science are concerned, they are great days so far as the material prosperity of our land is concerned— but they are *not* great days so far as the Church is concerned. Somehow or other the Church seems impotent, nerveless, helpless, and the reason for it lies here: we are neither cold nor hot, we are lacking in zeal, we have lost our moral enthusiasm; we play at religion; we touch it with our finger tips; we are content to patronize religion, and are not absorbed and possessed by it.

"Cold preaching," said Richard Baxter, "begets cold hearing." A cold church will always be confronted by an indifferent and callous world. "It is because we have so few high saints," said that same searching writer, "that we have so many low sinners."

Yes, it is because so few of us are "out and out" for Christ, it is because so few of us are wholly and entirely consecrated, it is because so few of us are possessed with a flaming and passionate zeal for God, that sin still exercises such terrible dominion over the hearts of multitudes of men and women. We need *zeal*—a high and sacred enthusiasm, the baptism of fire—and then we will go forth conquering and to conquer.

Simon, *the Zealot*, that is Simon's dignity and everlasting honor. He had a great and consuming zeal for God. To how many names in the church today could that same title be given? Could it be written after yours? Have you and I been zealous for God? Could you, with honesty and sincerity of soul, write your own name and then append to it this epithet—the zealot?

We can be zealous and enthusiastic enough over some things. We can be tremendously zealous in business; we give ourselves up body and soul to the making of money. We can be tremendously enthusiastic in politics; we take infinite pains to get our candidate elected. We can be tremendously keen upon our pleasures and amusements; we are quite ready to spend money and time upon them. We have become a nation of sports fanatics. But how many of us are zealous and enthusiastic for God and keen about the affairs of His Kingdom?

Let me ask it plainly: How many have been as zealous for God as they have been for their own business? How many have been as enthusiastic about the kingdom of Christ as they have about the success of their own political party? How many young people have been as keen about Christian service as they have about sports and pastimes? I say, how many? The truth is that God does not count for as much with most of us as does our business, or our politics, or our pleasures.

We are eager and enthusiastic about temporary things, but we are cold and listless and indifferent about the supreme things. I repeat again, that which we lack is zeal; we need enthusiasm, earnestness, eagerness in Christian work. We need the consuming ardor that won for Simon the epithet of Zealot. We need the sacrificial enthusiasm that made Paul count all things but loss for Christ. We lack the absolute consecration of soul that made Francis Xavier, the well-known "Patron of Foreign Missions," so effective. His heartcry was: "Yet more, O Lord, yet more!"

We need that consuming zeal that made the pioneer missionary to the American Indians, David Brainerd, agonize in prayer till he was wet with sweat, though he was kneeling in the shade. This zeal made him exult in the thought of any distresses that might come upon him in the advancement of Christ's kingdom on earth. We need that utter devotion to Christ's kingdom which made Henry Martyn leave Cambridge for India, there, as he put it, to let his life burn out for God.

When I read of these men and their burning zeal, I confess I am humbled and put to utter shame. Who of us has suffered for our enthusiasm for Christ? Who of us has ever agonized for souls? Who of us has let his life burn out for God? And yet I must add, until something of the passion that filled the hearts of Simon and Paul and Xavier and Brainerd and Martyn fills ours also, we will be impotent and helpless in face of an unbelieving world.

It is said that in England one of the Marquises of Lansdowne, distressed about the low moral condition of the town of Calne, in the early years of the past century, wrote to the vicar to ask him what steps ought to be taken to improve matters. "Send us an enthusiast," was the vicar's reply. That is exactly what the Church needs to become a victorious and triumphant Church; it wants *enthusiasts, zealots*—men and women who take their religion so earnestly that they are willing to be counted "fools" for Christ's sake. Yes, if Christians only put into their religion and Christian service the enthusiasm and zeal they now put into their business and their politics and their pleasures—the great Revival we long to see would soon be kindled.

So I covet for the Christian Church no gift more earnestly than I do Simon's fiery, eager and enthusiastic soul, and I know of no prayer we need more urgently to offer than this:

"Come, Holy Spirit, Heavenly Dove,
    With all Thy quickening powers,
Kindle a flame of sacred love
    In these cold hearts of ours."

Simon's Patriotism

The second thing Simon's title of *the Zealot* tells us about him is that he was *a Patriot*. The word ζηλωτής in Palestine, in addition to its broad and general meaning, came to have a special and distinctive meaning. It came to stand for those red-hot and flaming patriots who under Judas of Samala banded themselves together to deliver their country of Judaea from the Roman dominion. The "Zealots" were the "irreconcilables" of Judaea, hating the conqueror with a deep and unquenchable hatred, and ready at any moment to use the dagger and the sword against him. For the history of these zealots and the terrible ills they brought upon their own country I must refer you to the pages of Josephus.

Simon was just such a "zealot." He belonged to this irreconcilable party. He may have himself taken part in one or other of those terrible revolts that marked the course of the Roman rule in Palestine. He was a "patriot," ready to draw sword for his country, and if need be to die for her deliverance. Up to the time he met with Jesus that was Simon's idea of patriotism. His patriotism showed itself in a vehement desire to liberate his country from a foreign yoke, and that liberation he expected to bring about by dagger and sword.

When Simon became a disciple of Jesus he did not cease to be a patriot, but his patriotism took a deeper and nobler form. Under the teaching of Jesus he came to see that the great enslaving power in Palestine was not *Rome*, but *sin*; and so it came to pass that Simon flung away his dagger and sword and became instead a preacher of the Gospel of Jesus Christ. Thus Simon becomes to me a type both of the false and the true patriotism; he is a type in his preChristian days of that spurious patriotism that seeks to exalt a nation by sword and gun; he is in his later days a type of that noble patriotism that seeks to save the people from their sin and to establish a nation in righteousness.

Patriotism is a most noble and excellent virtue; but every good thing has its counterfeit, and so there are sham patriotisms abroad which every true lover of his country ought to denounce and repudiate. The state of feeling in our country at this time is very sensitive on this very subject of "patriotism." That patriotism which is boastful, arrogant, aggressive; which flings insults at foreign nations; which shrieks for war over every petty piece of territory; which clamors for bigger armies and larger fleets; that is a false patriotism, which will certainly lead any nation not to prosperity and power, but to disaster and utter overthrow.

Though at times we may seem to preach to deaf ears and unbelieving hearts, this is an eternal truth: force is no firm foundation for any nation's prosperity. Righteousness alone exalts a nation; and of nations as of individuals it is true—they that wield the sword will perish by the sword.

You find the true patriot not in the earlier, but in the later Simon—not in the sworn enemy of Rome, but in the sworn foe of Sin. This is the finest and higher patriotism—the patriotism that seeks to deliver a nation from its sins.

There never was a truer patriot than Isaiah. Read his prophecies, and you will see what his idea of patriotism was. The politicians were busy trying to strengthen the kingdom of Judah by alliances with this foreign nation and the other. Isaiah knew that the only way to make Judah strong was to have God on her side, and so this is the constant burden of his appeal: "Wash you, make you clean, put away the evil of your doing from before mine eyes; cease to do evil, learn to do well."

Paul loved his nation with a strong and deathless love. He was ready to become anathema, accursed for his kinsmen's sake according to the flesh. Turn to his letter to the Romans to see what Paul's idea of patriotism is. "Brethren," he writes, "my heart's desire and prayer for Israel is, that *they may be saved.*" Yes, that is the truest patriotism—the patriotism that seeks to save the people from their sins.

England had still nobler patriots than her soldiers and statesmen. If I had to mention those who had served England best, I would speak of John Wycliffe, the morning star of the Reformation, and of William Tyndale, the translator of the Bible, and of Hugh Latimer, the

Gospel preacher, and of John Wesley and George Whitefield, the great Evangelists of the eighteenth century.

It is the men and women who are seeking to save their countries from their sin who are the truest patriots. And it is this higher patriotism that I commend to you. We love our country, we love her with a respect more tender, more holy and profound than our own life. Let us show our love by grappling bravely with those terrible evils that threaten her. On both sides of the Atlantic let us show our love by carrying the Gospel to every nook and cranny of our land. Let us show our love by laboring to make our countries sober, pure and God-fearing. For "blessed is the nation whose God is the Lord, the people whom He has chosen for His own inheritance."

The Reconciling Power of Christ

Lastly, the presence in this list of the name of Simon the Zealot, the fierce and untamable patriot, is a beautiful illustration of the *reconciling power of Jesus Christ.* One mark of the kingdom of Jesus Christ is its *reconciliation.* Isaiah, foretelling that kingdom, told of the solution of old antagonism and the abolition of the most inveterate enmities. "The wolf," so he wrote in his beautiful and poetical speech, "also shall dwell with the lamb, and the leopard shall lie down with the kid; and the calf and the young lion and the fatling together; and a little child shall lead them. And the cow and the bear shall feed; their young ones shall lie down together, and the lion shall eat straw like the ox. And the sucking child shall play on the hole of the asp, and the weaned child shall put his hand in the viper den. They shall not hurt nor destroy in all my holy mountain" (Isaiah 11:6-9a).

The prophet's forecast is no lying vision. In the Kingdom of Christ all enmities will be abolished. In the first company of disciples Christ gathered about Him, in the circle of the Apostolate, you can see the prophecy fulfilled; you can see the wolf dwelling with the lamb and the leopard lying down with the kid. For in the list of the twelve you will find the names of two who were at daggers drawn—who hated one another with a fierce and bitter hatred, until Jesus drew both of them to Him, and so drew them to one another. Those two were Matthew the publican and Simon the zealot; Matthew the paid agent of the Roman power, and Simon its sworn foe; Matthew the recreant Jew and the instrument of the oppressor, and Simon the wild and turbulent patriot.

Simon and Matthew had been friends in the days of their youth. They had grown up together. It is possible they were related to one another. But when Matthew put on the uniform of Rome there was an end to their friendship. Friendship turned to a bitter hatred. Simon called Matthew a traitor; Simon spat on the name of Matthew; Simon was ready to plunge his dagger into Matthew's false and treacherous heart. If ever there seemed a hopeless and irreconcilable enmity, it was that which divided Simon the zealot from Matthew the publican.

But here are Matthew and Simon side by side, no longer strangers and aliens to one another, but friends and brothers. They have been reconciled to one another in Jesus Christ. And from the presence of Simon's name I gather fresh hope and confidence that the prophet's vision will yet be fulfilled, and that the time will come when they shall not hurt nor destroy in all God's holy mountain. He who bridged the gulf that separated Matthew from Simon can bridge every chasm that divides man from his brother man down to today. The world is torn and rent and seamed with divisions. Race, language, education, wealth—they all divide us. We are divided into nations hating and fearing one another, and sometimes taking upon ourselves the awful weapon of war. We are divided within the limits of one nation—into rich and poor, cultured and ignorant, capitalist and workman, and we regard one another with jealousy and dislike. I should despair of ever seeing that happy time of which Burns sings, when "Man to man the wide world o'er shall brithers be for a' that."

Our only hope lies in Jesus Christ. He alone can reconcile differences and remove antagonism. If ever the world is to be one, it will be one in Him. Christ is the great Reconciler. He reconciles man to God; He reconciles man to his brother. He has reconciled what seemed like hopeless antagonism. At His table rich and poor meet together and say, "Earth's poor distinctions vanish here." He bridged the gulf between master and slave, so that they turned to one another and said, "Beloved, if God so loved us, we ought also to love one another."

Our Savior obliterates distinctions of race and language, so that members of diverse nations regard one another as brothers in Christ. Yes, Jesus Christ is the great Unifier, and we learn to love one another as we learn to love Him. I heard of an old and white-haired man who was standing fascinated in a picture gallery before a picture of the Christ. After gazing at it a few moments he murmured, as if to himself, with face all aglow, "Bless Him, I love Him."

A stranger standing near overheard him, and said, "Brother, I love Him too," and clasped his hand. A third caught the sentence, and said, "I love Him too," and soon there was in front of that picture a little company of people with hands clasped, utter strangers to one another, but made one by their common love for Jesus Christ.

A common love to Christ will issue in the clasped hand between man and man and nation and nation. And so, with the noise of strife and the clash of arms in my ears, I yet look forward to the time when strife will end and wars will cease, when all the antagonisms and hates that divide and sunder people shall be utterly abolished—when every partitioning wall will be broken down, and every separating chasm will be filled up.

When will that happy time come? It will come, as the prophet says, "When the knowledge of the Lord has covered the earth as the waters cover the sea." The Christ who reconciled Matthew and Simon can reconcile anyone and everyone, so that there will be neither Jew nor Greek, neither bond nor free, but all will be one in Christ Jesus.

11

THE UNKNOWN APOSTLES

"James son of Alphaeus . . . Judas son of James. . . ."
—Luke 6:15 NIV

FIRST OF ALL I must put in a word of warning against some false and quite unwarranted identifications of this James and Jude. I find it calmly assumed by many writers that this James and Jude are the same James and Jude who wrote the Epistles that bear their names. And I find it further assumed by many writers that the James and Jude here mentioned are to be identified with the James and Jude mentioned by Mark in the third chapter of his Gospel as being brothers of our Lord.

There seems to be no basis in fact for either of these identifications. The Christian Church has witnessed many barren and foolish controversies in the course of the nearly twenty centuries of its existence, but the most barren and futile and utterly needless controversy that ever divided Christendom was the controversy with reference to the "brethren of our Lord." Controversy is always painful and deplorable, but of some controversies it can be said that there was a certain inevitableness about them, arising as they do from difficult and debatable passages of Scripture. But no such plea can be advanced in excuse for this controversy about the "brethren of our Lord." It did not spring from difficulties in the Scriptures. As a matter of fact, as Dr. Joseph B. Mayor says, the whole controversy is an illustration "of a contumacious setting up of an artificial tradition above the written Word." No, it did not spring from Scripture, but from sickly and morbid sentiment.

According to the church Father Jerome, even this James the son of Alphaeus, mentioned in the text, was one of the brothers of our Lord. That is to say, we find one of our Lord's brothers in the Apostolic company. But Scripture states quite distinctly that "His brethren did not believe on Him." Further, whenever they are mentioned they are mentioned as a body quite distinct and separate from the Apostles. And, once again, we happen to know that the occasion of the conversion of that particular brother who bore the name of James was a special appearance conferred on him by Jesus after His rising from the dead. No, the attempt to prove that the "brothers" of our Lord were only "cousins," and to identify them with the sons of Alphaeus, one of whom is mentioned in lists of Apostles, breaks down utterly and hopelessly. On the other hand, every Scripture reference agrees perfectly with the plain and natural interpretation that these men, James and Joses and Judah and Simon, mentioned by Mark, were true brothers, i.e. sons of Joseph and Mary. Christ is never spoken of as Mary's only son, but always as her first-born son—an epithet that implies that she had "other sons" beside. When we find James and Joses and Judah and Simon in constant company with Mary, and distinctly spoken of as "brothers" of our Lord, it is simple defiance of Scripture to understand the word otherwise than in its plain and obvious meaning. Every other theory, at bottom, springs from a sickly sentimental contempt for marriage and extravagant admiration for the celibate life.

The consequence of what I have said is that this James mentioned here is by no means to be identified with the James who was a brother of our Lord, and who afterwards became the leader of the Church at Jerusalem. Nor is this Jude to be identified with the Judah named by Mark in the list of our Lord's brothers. He was not the *brother* of James, as the Authorized Version puts it, and on which translation those commentators depend who make him one of the Lord's brethren. He was, as the R.V. translates it, the *son* of James.

From all this it follows that the James and Jude mentioned in this list of Apostles are not to be identified with the writers of the Epistles that bear their names. For the Epistle of James was almost certainly written by the better-known James, the brother of our Lord and the pastor of the Jerusalem Church; while the writer of the letter by Jude proclaims himself in the first verses of his Epistle as the brother of James, i.e. no doubt the well-known James of Jerusalem. So, as the result of my negative reasoning, we have arrived at this: that these two men, James and Jude, did *not* write the Epistles that bear their names, and are *not* the brethren of our Lord.

What, then, do we know about them? Absolutely nothing but their names, and the fact that Jude, in the Upper Room, asked Christ this question: "Lord, what is come to pass, that Thou wilt manifest Thyself unto us and not unto the world?" These two Apostles are mere names to us. Of their character, their achievements, their personal history we know nothing.

Their names have come down to us graven on the pages of the Gospel history, but they are as hopelessly sunk in obscurity as are the vast majority of those who sleep in our churchyards, though their names be preserved for us in granite and in marble. At first sight the obscurity of these Apostles seems to make it impossible to make them the subject of a sermon, and yet on second thoughts this obscurity itself is a noticeable thing, and has some important lessons to teach us. That is, so to speak, the mark of James and Jude—*their obscurity.* We know a little about every other member of the Apostolate. We know literally nothing about these two. All that can be said of them is that they were *hopelessly obscure men.* And it is to the obscurity, the utter and absolute obscurity, of James and Jude, and the lessons their obscurity teaches, that I would now call your attention.

Unrecognized Service

The first point I would make is this: that the occurrence of these two names in the Apostolic lists, without a single deed attached to either of them, reminds us of the great and almost tragic commonplace of life, that much *faithful, patient, humble service goes unrecorded and unnoticed of men.* "Of them which Thou hast given me," said Christ, "I have lost none save the son of perdition." Among the twelve there was only one false and faithless disciple and that was Judas Iscariot. As for the rest, they all gave to Jesus the faithful and devoted service of brave and loyal hearts.

They had differing gifts. Some were men of shining and conspicuous genius like Peter and John; others were men of small and humble talent like James and Jude. And yet I will be bold to say—and I have the words of the Master Himself to warrant me in saying it—that James and Jude served their Lord with as fine a fidelity as either Peter

or John. While the sayings and doings of Peter and John are recorded
for us in the Gospels and the Book of the Acts of the Apostles,
however, not a word is said about the equally faithful, though perhaps
not so striking, service of James and Jude. That is the world's way—
conspicuous service it notes, but lowly service rendered in humble
spheres it allows to pass unrecorded.

The unrecognized saints and heroes of earth are a vast host. It is
this thought of humble and heroic fidelity passing away unnoticed
that gives its pathos to Gray's immortal elegy as he muses in the
Churchyard—

> *"Perhaps in this neglected spot is laid*
> *Some heart once pregnant with celestial fire;*
> *Hands that the rod of empire might have swayed,*
> *Or waked to ecstasy the living lyre:*
>
> *Full many a gem of purest ray serene*
> *The dark unfathom'd caves of ocean bear;*
> *Full many a flower is born to blush unseen,*
> *And waste its sweetness on the desert air."*

Yes, every churchyard in the world contains the dust of men who
lived brave, heroic, faithful lives, but who are unknown to fame; and
among those "bravely dumb who did their deed and scorned to blot it
with a name," James the son of Alphaeus and Jude the son of James
must be reckoned. I can tell you nothing about them. I know of no
single achievement of theirs. I can just decipher their name on the
headstone in the great world's sleeping-place, and beneath each name
this sentence: "He hath done what he could."

This is what constitutes the real greatness of James and Jude—they
did their best, even though men did not notice them. They were faithful
even in a lowly place. It is comparatively easy to do one's best in a
conspicuous place. The mere fact that people watch our efforts and
speak of our work is in itself an incentive and a stimulus and an
encouragement. The hard thing is to do one's best when no one
watches and no one notices and no one praises. That is the triumph
and final achievement of fidelity.

Thank God some have been equal to this high feat! Some of the
best work ever done on this earth has been done by men and

women unknown to fame. I remember inspecting Lincoln Cathedral in the company of the late Precentor Venables. The old gentleman spoke with the utmost enthusiasm of the two towers that adorn the west front of that glorious edifice. He pointed out to me the beauties of the architecture and the extraordinary wealth and detail of the work, and then added quietly, "And no one knows who built them." Some of the finest work in Lincoln Minster is the work of an unknown builder. He did his faithful deed, and was content that men should forget him; but his work lives on, a thing of beauty and a joy forever.

Some of the best spiritual work in this world is done by faithful and humble souls—in the home, in the Sunday school class, in the tiny chapel. No one ever speaks of these workers. The great world does not even know their names. They did not labor for fame or applause. They labored out of love for their work and their Master.

Amongst those who attained to this high position of doing their very best in a small and humble sphere were these two Apostles—James and Jude. It did not bother them that people always talked of Peter or of John or of Paul and never spoke of them. They just went on doing their faithful best day by day, and saying to their souls, "Men love thee, praise thee, heed thee not. The Master praises, what are men?"

I do not know how you feel, but I stand rebuked by James and Jude, these men who were faithful in a very little. We are so eager for applause! We are so covetous of praise! We so like to have our every little service recognized, and often enough if the recognition is not forthcoming we decline to render the service!

Oh, that God would give us the spirit of James and Jude! Most of us occupy, comparatively speaking, humble spheres. We shall attain to no great fame. Our names will figure in no histories. Yet let us do our very best.

Yes, whether men praise or whether they ignore us, let us ask for grace to do our humble best so that upon our headstone that same verse may be written, "He hath done what he could," and upon our ears the commendation may fall, "Well done, good and faithful servant; thou hast been faithful in a few things, I will make thee ruler over many things: enter thou into the joy of thy Lord."

The Recognition of Heaven

The second point I will make is this: the names of these two Apostles remind us that, though faithful work and faithful workers may go unnoticed here, *both the work and the workers are remembered in heaven*. "There are first which shall be last," said our Lord, "and there are last which shall be first." Some of the unnoticed and neglected names of earth are amongst the glorious and familiar names of heaven. Amongst these are the names of these two obscure Apostles, James and Jude. I read this in the glowing description of the New Jerusalem in John's Apocalypse: the walls of the city had twelve foundations, and in them the names of the twelve Apostles of the Lamb. Yes, in walking round the city I notice on the foundations not only the names of the great four—Peter, James, John and Andrew alone—I notice also the names of these obscure Apostles, James and Jude. They share in the glory and honor of the greatest of the Apostles, for like them they had done their very best. In one of his letters Paul draws a sharp contrast between the condition of the saint here and above. "As unknown," he writes, "and yet well known"—"unknown" to the records of earth, but "well known" in the books of heaven; "unknown" to human society, but "well known" to the angels of God.

These two Apostles left no record of the work they did. We have no account of any books they wrote or any journeys they undertook, or any miracles they wrought, or any churches they founded. They are the "unknown" Apostles. Unknown, and yet "well known."

Their names are familiar names above; in the foundations of the city are the names of the *twelve* Apostles of the Lamb. And with James and Jude, these humbler Apostles whose names are graven on the foundations of the eternal city, as my text, I will preach the blessed and comforting truth, that *no faithful toil is ever overlooked or forgotten in heaven*.

"Full many a flower is born to blush unseen, and waste its sweetness on the desert air," wrote Thomas Gray, the noted English poet. When those lines come to be applied to *people* they are true only as far as this world is concerned. A sweet and gracious life may pass unnoticed of men, but it is seen of God. Its sweetness is not wasted on the desert air, for it comes up before God for an acceptable sacrifice, an odor of a sweet smell.

No service is ever overlooked of God, and the names of some of the humblest saints of earth are amongst the well-known names of heaven. "Unknown," yes; and yet (thank God!), "well known." There comes into my mind at this time the thought of one quiet individual who has labored for Christ with a fine and heroic fidelity in a very quiet corner of the Master's vineyard. He has been a village pastor all his days. His name never figures in denominational papers. His voice is never heard at the conventions of our church. He does not pose as one of its leaders. As far as the great public is concerned, he is to a large extent an "unknown" pastor. But I transport myself in imagination to the heavenly Jerusalem, and I find that the name of this man who has been so bravely faithful in a small sphere, who has spent his very life in ministering to the souls of humble village people is a familiar name amongst the angels.

And I will preach that same blessed truth to you my readers. You may be unknown on earth, and yet well known in heaven. No faithful toil, however humble, is ever overlooked. The work of the mother in the home, the teacher in his class, the preacher in the village chapel, may go unnoticed by the great world, but it is all down in the Lamb's Book of Life. Yes, everything is down in that wondrous Book.

Every kind word you have ever spoken, every gentle deed you have ever done, every visit to the sick and sorrowing you have ever paid, every cup of cold water you have ever held out to parched and thirsty lips—it is all down in the Book and it will be read out to your credit on the Great Day. Servants laboring in humble and quiet places, never cheered by the need of human praise, look away to the recompense of the reward that awaits you. Your toil is all recorded yonder, and you, the *unknown* of earth, may be among the "well-known" of heaven.

That, after all, is the place to be known. "Fame" has been called the last infirmity of noble minds. But I am not sure it is an *infirmity* at all. Everyone longs for fame. All want to be remembered. But let us make sure that we are seeking the true fame. "A peerage or Westminster Abbey!" cried Nelson. "I am painting for eternity," said a great French painter. But I can show you a more lasting fame than that which the French painter and the English sailor sought. Westminster Abbey will crumble into dust some day; painting, in process of time, must perish. But I can show you the way to an undying fame—have your names written in the Lamb's Book of Life. "The righteous shall

be had in *everlasting* remembrance." Yes, *that* is the Book on which to
have our names inscribed.

Some people would feel their ambition was fulfilled and fame
really theirs if their names came to be inserted in *Who's Who*. But the
names in those registers of earthly ranks and dignities change from
year to year, and the time is coming when the world, with all its
pomp, will dissolve, and, like some insubstantial pageant faded, leave
not a rack behind; and everyone who relies upon these things for
fame may as well write with John Keats, "Here lies one whose name
was writ in water."

No, the Book to have our names in is the Lamb's Book of Life.
That is to ensure undying fame. And the way to have our names
inscribed on that volume is faithfully to love and serve the Lord
Christ. The remembrance of such will never pass away. "He that
doeth the will of God abideth for ever."

The True Worker

One last point to remember: the silence of the Scriptures with
reference to these two Apostles suggests, as Dr. Maclaren says, that,
after all, the Apostles were not the real workers in the Church, but
Christ. Had the Apostles been all-important we should have had
minute and detailed accounts of their careers. As a matter of fact,
Scripture says little about even the chief of the Apostles, and some, as
James and Jude, it dismisses in absolute silence. The reason for this is
that the Bible wishes to concentrate attention upon Jesus Christ as
the all-important person.

A painter takes care not to let the accessories in his picture draw
attention away from the central figure. I once read a story of one of
the great painters who had painted a picture of the Last Supper. A
friend came one day to inspect this picture, and after gazing at it for
some time, said, "How beautifully those cups upon the table are
painted." The painter at once took up the brush and painted them
out. Turning to his dumbfounded friend, he said, "I want men to look
at the Christ."

In the same way the Gospels and the New Testament generally
point to Christ. They will not allow the figure of any man, not even
of a Peter or a Paul, to obscure the figure of Christ. What is Paul and
what is Apollos, and what, we may add, are Peter and John and James

and Andrew? They are ministers, through whom men believed and everyone as the Lord gave to him; they are but instruments through whom the Divine power made itself felt. It was not they who did the work; the excellency of the power was of God, and not of them. The real worker in the Church was Christ. So these two Apostles are just mentioned and then dismissed without a word. To emphasize them and their service would be to obscure the great fact that the Church depends not on its Apostles and preachers, but on its living and present God.

The real worker in the Church is Jesus Christ, and the power and conquering energy of the Church depend upon *Him*. There is infinite comfort in that truth. We are apt sometimes to magnify the importance of the human instrument. We lean upon our great preachers and leaders. And so, when a great preacher or leader is removed we become despondent and hopeless about the work. Remember, the real worker in the Church is *Christ.* Paul may plant, Apollos water, but God alone gives the increase. We thank Him for the great men, the princes in Israel whom He sends to us from time to time. But the work does not depend upon them. They pass away, but the work goes on.

The secret of the Church's power is the Church's Christ. He remains with us always, even to the end of the world. And it is because Christ is in His Church, and not because it numbers this and the other great man in its ranks, that we have the right to look forward to the happy day when the kingdom of this world will become the kingdom of our Lord and of His Christ.

12

JUDAS ISCARIOT

"After he had said this, Jesus was troubled in spirit and testified, 'I tell you the truth, one of you is going to betray me.'"
—*John 13:21 NIV*

OUR LORD HAD come to the very last night of His life. Before Him, only a few hours away, lay the Garden and the Judgment Hall and the Cross and the Grave. As He sat at supper with the twelve in the Upper Room that night, Jesus, according to John's testimony, was *troubled in spirit.* "What wonder," is our remark upon this statement of the Evangelist, "that Jesus was troubled in spirit!" The prospect of the bloody sweat and the spitting and the scourging and the nailing to the bitter tree was enough to make even the strong Son of God exceeding sorrowful even unto death.

But John's account seems to imply that it was none of these things that moved the Master. It was not so much the thought of His sufferings in the Garden or on the Cross that brought that look of pain into His face as He reclined at the Supper. No, it was not the thought of the agony in the Garden, or the shameful indignities of the Judgment Hall, or the cruel tortures of the Crucifixion that troubled Him. Rather, it was the thought of the *treachery of a friend.* "After he had said this, Jesus was troubled in spirit and testified, 'I tell you the truth, one of *you* is going to betray me.'"

The Ingratitude of Judas

"Blow, blow, thou winter wind," says Shakespeare, in one of the most familiar of his songs—

> *"Thou art not so unkind*
> *As man's ingratitude;*
> *Thy tooth is not so keen*
> *Because thou art not seen,*
> *Although thy breath be rude.*
> *Freeze, freeze, thou bitter sky,*
> *Thou dost not bite so nigh*
>   *As benefits forgot;*
> *Though thou the waters warp,*
>   *Thy sting is not so sharp*
>   *As friend remember'd not."*

Our Lord was to know the cruel bite of ingratitude, and it stung Him to the very quick. "The Son of Man shall be betrayed into the hands of men," He had said in solemn warning more than once. But the bitterness of the betrayal was rendered tenfold more bitter by the fact that it was brought about through the instrumentality of a *friend*.

"A man of sorrows and acquainted with grief," was the description of the Messiah given Isaiah centuries before Jesus was born in Bethlehem. And this is what our Savior was. He was a man of sorrows. He was acquainted with every grief that visits the human heart—except the sorrow and the grief for sin. The sorrow of a lonely life—He knew it; "His brethren did not believe on Him." The sorrow of disappointment—He knew it; "He came to His own and His own received Him not."

The sorrow of spurned and rejected love—He knew it; "how often would I have gathered thy children together as a hen gathereth her brood under her wings, and ye would not." The sorrow caused by the death of a loved one— He knew it; "Jesus wept." And that no sorrow incident to human life might be lacking, this further ingredient was added to our Lord's bitter cup—He was *betrayed and sold by a friend*. Brutus, when dying, could say—

> *"My heart doth joy that yet in all my life*
> *I found no man, but he was true to me."*

But it was not given to Jesus to be able to say even that. He chose twelve that they might be with Him. He offered to them His friendship. He admitted them into the very closest intimacy, lavishing upon them all the wealth of His tender and gracious love. And from that little circle of twelve came forth the man who was to sell Him.

"Did I not choose you, the Twelve, and one of you is a devil?" He asked. That was the peculiar bitterness in the death of Christ. It was brought about by the *instrumentality of a friend*. The hate of the priests, the furious clamor of the mob, the pitiful cowardice of Pilate, the brutality of the soldiers—Jesus could contemplate the prospect of it all with a quiet heart; but the thought that one of His own beloved and cherished twelve should sell Him to his deadly foes for a slave's ransom pierced Him to the quick.

"Mine own familiar friend," was the cry of His outraged heart, "in whom I trusted, who did eat of My bread, hath lifted up his heel against Me." "When Jesus had said this, He was troubled in His spirit, and testified and said, Verily, verily, I say unto you, that one of *you* shall betray Me." And the one who thus returned treachery for love and pierced his Master's soul was Judas Iscariot, the son of Simon.

About Judas' tragic story I need scarcely say a word—it is a familiar tale. Judas is remembered for one thing—he sold his Lord. You will find his name at the bottom of the Apostolic lists, and always attached to his name the crime which covers him with shame and everlasting contempt. Yes, Judas' name and his terrible sin are inseparably coupled together. "Judas Iscariot, which also betrayed Him," say Matthew and Mark. "Judas Iscariot, which was the traitor," says Luke.

Everything else about Judas has been forgotten except his crime and the fact that in remorse for the crime he had committed he went out and hanged himself. Scripture contains many a tragic tale. It tells the story of many a shipwrecked life. In its pages you find the history of a Lot who well-nigh lost his soul at Sodom; of a Samson who died making sport for the Philistines; of a Solomon falling away in his old age to worship idols. But Lot, Samson and Solomon are nothing compared with Judas. Never was a tale so tragic as his. Never was shipwreck so terrible as his. We read the story of this man who sold his Lord for thirty pieces of silver, and then went out and hanged himself, and we can understand that austere and stern word of our Lord's, "Better were it for that man if he had not been born."

How Judas Came to Be an Apostle

The presence of the name of Judas in the lists of the twelve gives rise to several questions which are more easily asked than answered. This is the first question I would ask: *How did Judas become an Apostle at all?* This is what Mark says about the choosing of the twelve: "And Jesus appointed twelve that they might be with Him, and that He might send them forth to preach." Jesus picked out these twelve men to be His chosen friends and to be preachers of His Gospel. The choice of Peter we can understand, and the choice of John and James, and indeed of all the eleven down to the obscure Apostles James and Jude. But why did Jesus give a place among His intimates to this man Judas, who also betrayed Him?

There are some who maintain that Jesus chose Judas because He knew he was a traitor—that He chose him for that very purpose. A.B. Bruce says, "Iscariot was chosen merely to be a traitor, as an actor might be chosen to play the part of Iago." But this seems a monstrous and incredible theory, and I for one unhesitatingly reject it.

There are others who agree that *Jesus was deceived in Judas*—that He took him for a better man than he was. This theory would explain everything if we could accept it. The choice of Judas would be perfectly intelligible if at the time of his choice Jesus really thought he was a good man. But could Jesus be deceived in that way? I am not prepared to assert that Jesus was *omniscient* in the common understanding of the word. When He laid His Godhead by "He emptied Himself," Paul says. He placed voluntary limitations upon Himself. He laid aside this and the other Divine prerogative. And among other things He laid aside the Divine omniscience.

There are some things about which our Lord during His earthly sojourn confessed Himself ignorant. But Scripture seems specifically to forbid our thinking that He was deceived in Judas. For not only do we find in the fourth Gospel the general statement that Jesus knew what was in man, but we find also the definite and particular statement that "Jesus knew *from the beginning* . . . who it was that should betray Him." The fact of it is, I can see no full and complete answer to the question, which, as Dr. Plummer says, "runs up into the insoluble problems of the origin of evil and of Divine omniscience, combined with human free will."

I am unable to answer the question, "Why did Jesus choose Judas?" to my own complete intellectual satisfaction, while I am bound to admit myself here in the presence of a great mystery, yet this must also be said: to all outward appearance at the time of his calling Judas seemed as likely a man for an Apostle as any one of the twelve. That must have been so when you think of it.

The choice of Judas seems to have struck nobody as strange. No one protested against the selection of Judas. Right to the end no one seems to have had a suspicion of him. Apparently he was a pattern of piety. He seemed as earnest and as enthusiastic and as devoted as any one of his colleagues, so that the choice of Judas seemed to all who knew of it a most fitting and proper choice.

This further I will add: at the time of his choice Judas' fervor and enthusiasm were no sham. At the beginning this man was no conscious and deliberate hypocrite. I believe when Judas became a disciple he was sincere in his discipleship; I believe he was honest in his desire to serve and follow Christ. The mischief with Judas was not that he was not sincere, but that he was not whole-hearted in his devotion.

Judas did not leave *all* to follow Christ. He offered to his Master only a divided allegiance. For before the days of his discipleship Judas had allowed the love of money to creep into his soul. He had begun to toil and sweat and slave for money. Like Matthew the publican, Judas, away at Kerioth, was ready to do almost anything for money. And when he entered the service of Jesus Christ, Judas brought this love of money with him.

He was what the Apostle James, in a fine phrase, calls a "double-minded man." He had a divided heart, a twofold love. He tried to do the impossible—to serve both mammon and God at the same time. And the tragedy of Judas' life roots itself just here. He made his bed in hell because he did not give his Lord his undivided heart.

Up to the time of their calls, the life histories of Matthew the publican of Capernaum and Judas the man of Kerioth ran on parallel lines, but all the distance between heaven and hell separated them at the finish. Matthew, when he was called, left his toll booth, his books, his *all* and followed Christ, and so became Matthew the holy Evangelist. On the other hand, Judas, when he was called, brought with him and still cherished in his heart his love of gold, and so became Judas, "which also betrayed Him."

With Judas as my text, I will preach the danger of a *divided heart*. "The double-minded man is unstable in all his ways," says James. He always stands on the edge of a precipice, and you never know when the fall may come. That is what so many of us offer to the Lord in these days—we offer Him a *divided* heart. We ask Him to share the dominion with money and pleasure, or some other of the world's delights. When we enter His service we bring with us some alien love. We do not give up *all* for Christ. We retain some lust, some desire, some secret sin, and in excuse for it say, "Is it not a little one?"

Is that not so? We must look into our own hearts at this moment and see. How many of us can honestly say that in our hearts there is no love but the love of Jesus? How many of us can honestly say we are "ever, only, all for Christ"? How many of us can claim to possess hearts "where only Christ is heard to speak, where Jesus reigns alone"? How many of us? As a matter of fact, have we not all *divided* hearts? Is there not in every heart something that disputes the dominion with Christ?

And yet, I warn you that the divided heart is a source of peril and infinite danger. For sin has a trick of growing—of growing until it hurls you from your place and places you in a pit of infamy and shame. Had anyone told Judas on the day of his call that someday he would sell the Christ for thirty pieces of silver, he would have answered in indignant horror at the bare suggestion, "Is thy servant a dog that he should do this thing?" But he kept a sin in his heart, and this sin grew until it drove him to commit that monstrous and unspeakable crime. Beware what you cherish in your hearts—for lust when it is conceived brings forth sin, and sin when it is full grown brings forth death! And lest you, too, should share Judas' tragic fate, let this be your daily, urgent, and most importunate prayer: "O God, Who hast put in my heart the love of Thy Son Jesus Christ, deliver me in Thy great mercy from every other love, and *unite* my heart to love and fear His name."

The second question that suggests itself in connection with Judas' tragic story is this: "What were the motives for the betrayal?"

Why Did Judas Betray Jesus?

The Scripture says that Judas *sold* Jesus to the priests for thirty pieces of silver. But many have felt that greed was insufficient explanation of the crime. Thus, various theories have been invented to account for the betrayal. Some would have us believe that the betrayal was after all not the terrible sin the Church has always held it to be, but only a tragic blunder, and a blunder made with virtuous intent.

Some scholars have represented Judas as a vehement, impatient, but well-meaning partisan, who sold Jesus to the priests simply in order to compel Him to declare Himself—take unto Himself His great power and reign. I am not going to waste my time or yours in disproving this theory. It has been popularized in books of fiction; but all that needs to be said about it is this: it is absolutely contradictory of and antagonistic to the whole teaching of Scripture. The Gospels never represent the crime of Judas as a blunder, and Judas himself as a blunderer. The Scriptures regard Judas' deed as a veritable mystery of iniquity, and Judas himself it brands as a traitor and a devil.

But others who refuse to apologize for Judas feel the necessity of discovering some other motive for the crime than that of mere greed for those thirty pieces of silver. Dr. Patrick Fairbairn attributes the deed to Judas' resentment at Christ's failure to establish a Messianic kingdom of temporal power, and Dr. A.B. Bruce attributes it to the hatred which took possession of Judas' heart when he realized that Jesus read him through and through, and saw his hypocrisy and wickedness. Others, again, say that Judas betrayed Christ to save himself—that he saw disaster impending, and so turned, as we should say, "King's evidence."

All these motives may perhaps have played their part. But I am going to take my stand on the plain word of Scripture, and maintain that what prompted him to this crime was *greed*. "He was a thief," says John, "and pilfered from the common purse." Greed had already made him a thief—in the end it made him a traitor. So consuming became his desire for gold that he turned His Lord in for money and sold Him to His foes for thirty pieces of silver.

Those who object that Judas' avarice is not a sufficient motive, forget what men will do for money. For money men will sell honor and truth; for money parents will sell their children; for money women will sacrifice themselves on the altar of brutal lust. Ezekiel speaks of "polluting God for handfuls of barley and for pieces of bread." Amos speaks of "selling the righteous for silver and the poor for a pair of shoes." In these days men and women barter away their souls for money. They sacrifice religion and their hope of heaven for money, so that I find no difficulty in believing that, driven by his terrible and consuming lust for gold, Judas, nearly twenty centuries ago, sold his Lord for thirty pieces of silver.

And now, leaving the motives of the crime, what shall we say of the crime itself? Well, this first. It was a—

Sin against Privilege

If ever a man had a chance to become a saint, that man was Judas. For two years at least this man lived with Christ. He was privileged to listen to Christ's wonderful words, to behold His marvelous deeds, and to witness His beautiful life. Never in all the world's history was there a man who had a better chance than Judas! We are told in these days that what a man becomes depends largely on his environment. Let a man live amid filthy and vicious surroundings, and he will grow up filthy and vicious; let a man live amid clean and healthy surroundings, and he will grow up clean and healthy. It is a neat and handy theory. The only drawback to it is that *it is not true.* According to that theory Judas, living for two years in closest intimacy with the One sinless and perfect Being who ever walked earth, ought to have grown daily better and nobler and holier. But that is not how the story reads.

Instead of Judas becoming a saint, the devil entered into his heart and he went away and sold his Lord for thirty pieces of silver.

Religious privileges are powerless to save a man. "Thou Capernaum, art thou exalted unto heaven?—thou shalt be brought down to Hades." "Then," says Bunyan, in the last sentence of his Dream, "I saw that there was a way to Hell even from the gates of Heaven." Yes, from the very gates of Heaven! For surely if ever a man stood at the gates of Heaven, Judas stood there when he was the friend and companion of Christ. But there is a way to Hell even from the gate of Heaven, and *Judas found it.*

I believe the character of Judas is in the old Book to warn us against trusting to the religious privileges we enjoy. We have been lifted high even to the gates of Heaven in privilege. With our open Bibles and our places of prayer, and our Gospel liberty, none have been so highly exalted as we. And yet, in spite of them all, we may be brought down to hell. "Wherefore let him that thinketh he standeth take heed lest he fall."

No, I will venture further, not only to say that Judas sinned in spite of privilege, but that *privilege hardened him in sin.* Because Judas did not profit by the fellowship of Christ, he was the worse for it. For that double effect always attends contact with Christ. It is either a blessing or a curse. Fire softens wax, but it hardens clay; air nourishes the growing plant, but it helps to corrupt and destroy the cut flower. So the influence of Jesus that changed the fickle Peter into the man of rock and the hot-tempered John into the Apostle of Love, was making Judas capable of the most dastardly crime of history. Yes, the very purity and holiness of Jesus did but harden Judas and intensify his hatred of the good he saw but would not follow. The day came that in the madness of his hate he betrayed Jesus to a cruel death. And Judas teaches us that same solemn lesson. Privileges unused become curses. It is good to meet every Lord's day, to have God's Word read and His Gospel preached. But unless you mean to obey the Word, you would be better off never to have seen a Sunday dawn. You had better not have entered the place of prayer; for while the Word accepted and obeyed is the savor of life unto life, that same Word rejected and disobeyed becomes the savor of death unto death.

Sin against Warning

To go further, this sin of Judas was a sin against *repeated warnings.* Judas did not rush blindly and ignorantly to his fate. Jesus saw the peril that threatened His disciple's soul, and again and again the warning note was sounded. You have noticed how Christ returns in His speech to the love of money and its perils to the soul. Nothing looms so largely in the teaching of our Lord.

It is astonishing to take a pencil and mark in the Gospels every reference to money and every warning against it. Have you ever asked yourself why Jesus said so much about money? I will tell you. Partly because the sin of loving money was so prevalent, but partly because He also saw that same terrible sin working its ruin and havoc in one of his own disciples' heart. Yes, these multitudinous sayings about money are just evidences to me of Christ's concern and anxiety for Judas' soul.

It was to Judas He said, "Ye cannot serve God and mammon." It was at Judas He looked when He said, "What doth it profit to gain the whole world and lose one's life?" It was for Judas' benefit He spoke the parable of the man who had his barns and storehouses full, but who had an unprepared soul.

Yes, Judas was faithfully warned; but in spite of all he clung to his sin, until for it he was ready to sacrifice his Lord. We too, when we sin, sin against warning. We are not left in ignorance of the issues and results and consequences of sin. Did we sin in ignorance, we might cry to a merciful God to have pity on us; but what excuse will we plead when we continue in sin against pleading and entreaty and warning?

A Repeated Sin

The last word I shall say about Judas' sin is this: it is a *sin often repeated*. We imagine that the betrayal and crucifixion of Christ only took place once, and that Judas' sin is unique and solitary in its enormity. No, this is an oft-repeated sin. It is true that there are now no high priests to pay out silver to us; it is true there is no actual nailing the body of Christ to the bitter tree. But Christ is still sold, and Christ is still crucified afresh.

Yes, let me say it again. We still sell Christ, and *we* crucify Him afresh. We shudder with horror at the crime of Judas, and yet sometimes I feel that instead of pointing the finger at Judas, I ought to go and stand in the same pillory with him as guilty of the same shameful and unspeakable sin.

"One of you," said our Lord, with anguish in His voice, "shall betray Me." "One of *you*." Those eleven disciples, knowing the weakness and sin of their own hearts, were smitten with a terrible fear, and they looked at their Master with white faces, and said, "Lord, is it I?" There was not one there who said, "That is meant for Judas." Every man looked into his own heart, and seeing what a bottomless pit his heart was, every one felt *he* might be the traitor. Hence the question that came in tremulous accents from blanched lips, "Lord, is it I?"

When I hear Christ say still, "One of you shall betray Me," I too cry, "Lord, is it I?" For the heart I carry within me is a bottomless abyss. "Who can understand his errors?" asks the Psalmist. Who really knows what enormities he may be guilty of? Who knows what possibilities for evil lay latent within?

This much I know: we find it easy still to sell Christ; we sell Him to succeed in business; we sell Him for pleasure; we sell Him for social position. We crucify Him afresh, and put Him to an open shame by forgetting Him, repudiating His authority, bringing disgrace upon His name. "One of *you*," He says to us, "shall betray Me."

This week one of us could turn traitor. I cannot treat that warning as if it were not meant for me. Like the disciples, knowing my own weakness, I know that one may be myself. All I can do is to give myself and this treacherous heart of mine into the keeping of Almighty Love, and pray with the Psalmist, "Keep back Thy servant from presumptuous sins; let them not have dominion over me. Then shall I be upright, and shall be innocent from the great transgression." This is the lesson I have learned as I have looked at the life of the traitor, Judas Iscariot.